What People Are Saying Ab [barcode: MW00581634]

"Ms. Regina DuBose has written an easy-to-read way to get started with Jesus. She takes us on her personal journey in search of persons, events, reflections and prayers that helped her to connect with Jesus. She hopes to help her readers use similar experiences in their own lives to make the journey their own.

This is not a heavy theological tract with technical terms that leaves people wondering if it's really that hard to find Jesus. It is a way to use every-day experiences with people, events and resources to center oneself in God.

Anyone with a desire to connect with Jesus needs to read this spirit-filled 'way' discovered by Regina DuBose."

—**Fr. Norman Paul Thomas**, *Pastor, Sacred Heart Catholic Church*

"In her newest, but not last publication of *Getting Started with Jesus,* Regina expresses and exposes the core necessities of beginning, nurturing, maintaining, and maturing in her walk with the Lord Jesus Christ. As so many have been great starters, but not great finishers, Regina provides the plan and process of discovering your individual and collective purpose as it relates to your walk with God to ensure a successful journey despite personal setbacks, temptations, and the grace God provides to return even after we've strayed off the path. She shows us how sound doctrinal teaching, providential partnerships, and prophetic preaching plays a critical role in the life of those called to be in the world but not of the world. The insight and wisdom received from her life and experiences as a born-again, Blood-bought, baptized believer will encourage anyone who has accepted or is considering a life-long journey with Jesus! This book will be a blessing to you and is a biblically inspired roadmap to keep God at the forefront as Guard, Gauge, and Guide as you go through life! #enjoythejourney"

—Rev. Dr. Lee C. Winfrey, *Pastor, Partakers Church Baptist*

"In *Getting Started with Jesus,* Regina DuBose has created a book which is part personal journal, part treatise and part Bible Study. As they combine, the book becomes an engaging introduction to a powerful perspective on taking Christianity personally and seriously. This is a valuable contribution to contemporary conversation about what it means to be a 'Christian' and what it means to be 'evangelical.'

Weaving in stories about her personal faith journey, Ms. DuBose assures her readers that she is not writing from the perspective of one who has not endured the 'trials, tribulations and tests' about which she writes. The work of a former counselor and Sunday School teacher, her book is enlightening about the faith, encouraging for those struggling, and challenging for anyone who has been taking their faith walk a little too lightly.

Using a methodical approach to a life of faith, Ms. DuBose walks along with the reader through the stages of Christian maturity, 'Starting,' 'Growing,' 'Staying' and 'Living' as if she were walking along with one of the pregnant teens she once counseled.

Ms. DuBose is clear that this book is not intended to be merely informational. It is also intended to be inspirational, giving direction to those who may be seeking, either outside or within the church, a closer, more meaningful relationship with Jesus of Nazareth. I encourage those who have not yet found that personal connection to Jesus to share in this experience of one who has."

—**Dr. Kevin M. Turman,** *Retired Pastor, Second Baptist Church of Detroit*

"DuBose has written a unique narrative that specifically chronicles her walk to spirituality. She uses painful and sometimes distressing events to contextualize them in biblical references.

She includes vignettes of iconic people in her life who supported and helped to initiate choices and decisions she made that have directed her to where she is today. The scriptural references are especially significant and inspirational.

Some passages transition from being self-reflective to being instructive for others. DuBose's passion for ministry is clearly evident in sections throughout her writing. These can provide instructive messages for her audience; and can foster or serve as an incentive for further biblical study."

—**Esther M. Coleman, PhD.,** *Marygrove College*

"Ms. DuBose has always been an energetic, gifted person. She is an all-around balanced Christian. She is musically inclined, and also biblically controlled by the Word of God. She is always respectable to her peers and the Unity Baptist Church.

Whatever group she has labored with in the church, she has been a great supporter from the kindergarten age to the season saints. Ms. DuBose is a worshipper in signing music, a Bible student, and a worker in evangelism ministry. She is an amazing young lady who has persevered through all of her trials and tribulations. She has guided her daughter's education, seeing that she has attended some of the best schools offered.

She is a young lady of tremendous faith. She is a businesswoman who launched out as an entrepreneur. As a black young lady, she took charge to start a business of her own, by the grace of God. In business, she has produced products that give distinction and significance to all walks of life.

Lastly, she possesses many gifts that one would not see because she doesn't brag or exalt herself. Ms. DuBose spends time exalting the Lord Jesus Christ. She gives all glory to God for all of her endeavors. Continue to be a blessing beyond these years in serving the Lord and the community.

"Christ in you, the hope of glory!" (Colossians 1:27)

May God's Riches Blessings Be Upon You."

—**Pastor & Mrs. Valmon D. Stotts,** *Unity Baptist Church,* 1996

Getting Started With Jesus

The Process for Spiritual Growth and Maturity

Regina A. DuBose

ATKINS & GREENSPAN
PUBLISHING

Copyright Page
Copyrighted Material
GETTING STARTED WITH JESUS:
The Process for Spiritual Growth and Maturity
Regina A. DuBose
Copyright © 2021 PERFECT PEACEWORKS, LLC
All Rights Reserved.

No part of this publication may be reproduced, stored in a retrieval system
or transmitted, in any form or by any means—electronic, mechanical,
photocopying, recording, or otherwise—without prior written permission
from the publisher, except for the inclusion of brief quotations in a review.

For information about this title or to order other books and/or
electronic media, contact the publisher:

Atkins & Greenspan Publishing
TwoSistersWriting.com
18530 Mack Avenue, Suite 166
Grosse Pointe Farms, MI 48236

ISBN 978-1-945875-90-8 (Hardcover)
ISBN 978-1-945875-91-5 (Paperback)
ISBN 978-1-945875-92-2 (eBook)

Printed in the United States of America

All of the stories in this work are true, however the names have
been changed to protect the privacy of individuals.

Scripture quotations are from the King James Version of the Bible.

Cover and Graphic Design: Ajani Winston and Van-garde Imagery, Inc.

Photo credit for author photo: Anita Bonnie Harrell

All photographs used with permission.

Photo credit for images of "The Versatilities" singing group:
Deborah Jameen Love-Peel.

Photo credit for photos of Regina DuBose at
Partakers Church Baptist, Detroit, Michigan: Anita Bonnie Harrell.

All uncredited photographs courtesy of Regina A. (Hinkle) DuBose
Family Collection and The Alexis Company Collection.

Dedication

To my parents, Samuel Matthew and Rosie Lee Hinkle; teachers at Hanneman Elementary, especially Mrs. Jaquetta Crews in sixth grade; my Spiritual Mother, Mrs. Margo DeRamus, who shaped my personal development, taught me to love others, and influenced my spiritual growth and maturity; and to Rev. Dr. Lee C. Winfrey and his wife Kimberly, who encouraged me to dream, again.

Contents

Living for Jesus

Introduction

THERE COMES A TIME in everyone's life when we have to ask, "Where is God in my life?" This question comes up over and over again at various stages of our development. Depending on how, when, and why we answer it will dictate a course in life. Whether during adolescence, at a high school debate, inside a college dormitory, or at a local dinner setting after work, we are faced with choosing an answer. Sometimes we're forced to ponder the question when a crisis occurs, or at the death of a beloved friend or relative. It may come up during times of sickness, at a time when someone loses their job, during the proceedings of a distasteful divorce, and in the midst of many other significant, critical events that tend to wear us down.

The journey of life continues and we must learn to function in our best behavior, dealing with one challenge at a time. Yes, in many cases, we ask ourselves, "Where is God in my life...now? Can this be real? What's happening here?" And, no matter how much we know, or how much we have, the case for man's inability to battle the unknown is obvious. We have no power over the future, our present is often very dismal, and we constantly wrestle with living in the past. We start, stop, start again, wait, change our minds, start all over, and then finally we succumb and think, *It's time. I have got to get closer to the one who knows everything... God.*

For me, I was 10 years old going on 11, when my parents sought the need to provide Godly training in our home by becoming affiliated with a local church. At the time in 1968, I don't know what my parents were thinking, but the 1967 riot of Detroit had occurred, and Rev. Dr. Martin Luther King, Jr. had been assassinated. People in the neighborhood, which bustled with young families, spent Sunday mornings preparing for church, then coming home for dinner. We lived in a close-knit community, but some of the Polish families were starting to move elsewhere and things were beginning to change. My brothers and I were immediately indoctrinated with God, Jesus Christ, the need for Salvation, and church attendance to make one's life better and meaningful. We began attending a local church recommended by my Dad's best friend.

It was an amazing experience as I watched my mother, father, and two older brothers (Junior and Ronnie) walk down the aisle, shake the preacher's hand, say they believed in Jesus and that they "join the church." My brothers became members of the choir, which was filled with young teenagers. They had their own special name, "The Choraleers." I sat next to my mother during the morning services, swinging my legs, (in between pinches) that were too short to touch the floor. I had to sit still, refrain from chewing gum, and obey the rules of church etiquette for little girls (by the way), that was strictly enforced by my mother's hands. My dad joined the Senior Usher Board. A big responsibility—uniform, badge, and all.

Finally, on one Sunday afternoon, as we were sitting around the dining room table, eating our dinner, I asked, "What do you have to do to sing in the choir?"

My mother replied, "Regina, you just can't sing in the choir, you have to join the church."

"Junior and Ronnie are in the choir and they can't even sing!" I replied.

She went on to explain the purpose and reason for church involvement as a member of God's family. However, in the back of my mind, I already knew that I was planning to "join the church" at the next opportunity, when they said, "The doors of the church are now open." I couldn't wait to get my opportunity.

There was a great soloist in the environment of our new church home. They called her Mrs. Johnnie Mae Jones. Every time this woman sang, the entire church was ecstatic! She had an electrifying voice with such depth and magnitude that made you feel as if you were standing in the "presence of God." Such power! Mrs. Jones often sang a solo or led a song right before the preacher got up to speak. When he would wind down the major points of his sermon, his voice would get really loud and emotional. Many times, as this was happening, different women in the church would start screaming, shouting, and hollering "Amen." It really frightened me, and this scene was my cue to leave. At that moment in the service, I would ask my mother, "Can I go downstairs?" We had a silent agreement, and she knew that I hated this part of the service because it literally scared the wits out of me. She would politely nod, "Yes."

There was nothing downstairs, no children's church or youth program, at that time. But we had a vending/pop machine, and some church material to read. Kids were always playing or wandering around until the service upstairs ended. I was always happy to see my family after church, and that everyone was fine.

On one particular Sunday, Mrs. Jones got up to sing a song called, "How Big is God?" (This is **still** my favorite song today). I really understood the words and meaning of that song, and she sang it beautifully. So, I politely got out of my seat, before my mother could pull me back, and proceeded down the aisle to join the church. For some strange reason, I didn't go downstairs on that particular Sunday, but sat in the sanctuary next to my mother for the entire sermon. My father was ushering at the time. As I made my way to the altar, listening to the meaningful words of that song, my whole demeanor and attitude changed by the time I made it to the front of the congregation. I reached out to shake the preacher's hand. With my eyes filled with tears, I gained a sense of God's presence in my spirit as I said, "Yes, I believe in this Jesus Christ." And so, my journey began at this local church along with my wonderful family.

Overview of the Christian Life

The chaos in the world today is quite evident. We see it promoted through crime, corruption, confusion, and man's inhumanity to man. Day after day, year after year, the world presents horrendous situations and circumstances to us from childhood to our senior years. We confront them, accept, and have to deal with issues throughout this journey that we call "life."

We are often convinced to walk in fear, wandering aimlessly, wondering about things, and worrying about an uncertain future. We hear many stories that emerge to the surface and attempt to dominate our thinking, our actions, and our productivity. Taking all of this into consideration, I believe it is futile to imagine a progressive, encouraging, and positive lifestyle, without a viable relationship with God the Father, God the Son, and God the Holy Ghost. We all seek to have a meaningful life with purpose, hope, ingenuity, stamina, and direction as a way of experiencing a true sense of satisfaction with our own personal journey. The questions you have to ask yourself throughout this reading are, "Where am I right now, where am I going, and where do I want to end up as my life unfolds? Am I truly satisfied?"

Well, just how do you get to God? "Jesus saith unto him, I am the way, the truth, and the life; no man cometh unto the Father, but by me." That's it in a nutshell. Jesus is the only way to God. He is the real way. He is the only way. He is not a way, or a better way. **He is the way.** This verse is in the New Testament of the Holy Bible, in the book of St. John 14:6, King James Version (KJV). As human beings, we try all kinds of things to get close to God. We do things to please God and to appease God. We perform good deeds, give away our material possessions and money, try to help out our friends, and so on. We tend to believe that these different acts of kindness will earn us "brownie points," with a holy, righteous, Almighty God.

Unfortunately, the more you do from this position, the further behind you're placed in the true line of God's infinite blessings. It's time to get your Christian journey on the right path, to experience joy, peace, blessings, understanding, and harmony in your personal relationship with God. This is one trip you will never forget and never regret. I'm a witness!

Getting Started With Jesus was written with you in mind. It is my own proclamation, testimony, and verification of the power of the Word of God when you **apply it** to your life problems. There are four major sections of the book within the eight chapters: 1) Getting Started With Jesus; 2) Growing In Jesus; 3) Staying With Jesus; and 4) Living for Jesus. Throughout the reading, there are examples of how I was doing at that point in my Christian life.

There are significant dates and details of some critical events. Those moments forced me to examine my progress, or fall out and regress in my walk with God.

The formula for this writing was derived from the Bible Study lessons that I had with an older woman whom I called "my Spiritual Mother." Her name was Margo. We met in our local neighborhood church during my early years as a "young member" of the Senior Choir. I was 18 years old at the time, and the choir for teenagers/young adults had disbanded.

Her goal was to make disciples for Jesus Christ by teaching people to teach, who teach others to teach, and duplicating that model. It was her desire to see people grow spiritually in their Christian walk, and be led to serve God in some capacity.

She held individual Bible sessions and our group session, which initially consisted of several young women who decided to commit their lives to Jesus Christ and live according to Godly principles. It was named, "The Fellowship." She started with a Christian book called *Learning to Be a Woman*, by Kenneth George Smith (1970), along with the Holy Bible as we began this journey.

Eventually, young men were "allowed" into the group, which presented an entirely new dimension and flair to all of us. This led to a deeper understanding of the roles in male/female relationships, according to the standards of Godly living.

The power dynamic of this group called "The Fellowship" is that one woman who was concerned about young people learning basic, Godly principles at that moment in time, was so important to her, that she opened the doors of her home, faithfully, for more than 40 years to teach and share this information with us. When her time on earth was about to end, I thought about the wonderful relationship that I had had with her, and now maintain with God, and the impact that she had on my spiritual growth and development as a Christian woman. As I went through the ups and downs, the growing pains, while facing life challenges, she was a special blessing to me: always sharing, caring, giving her time, loving, and teaching from her heart everything that God had placed inside her to offer.

Getting Started With Jesus will give you the additional faith, belief, strength, discipline, and hope that you need to help you determine and maintain worthwhile goals in life. However, the keyword is **choice.** We have to make a decision to accept Jesus Christ into our lives and to live according to His standards. God does not force Himself into our lives. We choose to let Him in. He gives us the option to choose or to reject Him. Simply put, man is a spirit that lives in all women, men, boys, and girls. He lives in a body. And he has a soul. It is recorded in John 3:16, "For God so loved the world, that he gave his only begotten Son, that whosoever believeth in Him should not perish, but have everlasting life." The next verse (17) says, "For God sent not his Son into the world to condemn the world, but that the world through him might be saved." After you accept Christ, you begin to grow in the Word of God. No doubt, you'll face hardships. That's the fact of life. But, the power of God helps you stay focused and leads you to an abundant life.

This book is a summation of what it takes to live a Godly life in such a wicked world today. It is also my personal tribute to Margo and the many people that God placed into my life to help me along the way. May your heart and mind be encouraged to live for Jesus, and share Godly teachings with others, as you delve into these principles which promote Jesus Christ as the more excellent way.

I hope that my book reveals a fresh start for you and those who may find themselves wondering why they have not received the fullness of Living for Jesus. You've come this far, so you must be ready. Well, let's get started with Jesus! It's the ultimate journey of a lifetime. God's been waiting just for you!

Be Peaceful,

Regina Alexis (Hinkle) DuBose

Getting Started

Chapter 1

Jesus & Me, The Relationship

"Girl, I just joined the church," a woman declares.

"Yeah?" her friend responds.

"Really, I walked down the aisle, shook the preacher's hand," the woman continued, "and I said, 'Yes, I believe in this Jesus!' You know, I think I'm gonna join that choir. They sound really good!"

"Amen, you go, girl!" her friend says.

Does this sound familiar?

Well, that's exactly how many people talk when they describe the beginning of their Christian journey. But, isn't it more? So much more? More than just a walk, and a handshake, and a formality of saying, "I believe in Jesus." And, more than just *going* to church Sunday after Sunday, year after year, program after program, with a special event here and a special event there, and oh yeah, every now and then someone else *joins* the church.

Look, before you know it, they've spent 20 or more years in the same old church, doing the same old things, in the same old way, with the same old people, who are really aging rapidly. Yet, they are facing the same old problems, circumstances, and issues that existed and were vividly present before saying, "Yes, I believe in Jesus Christ."

The relationship between God and mankind through Jesus Christ is fabulous, but many Christians barely scratch the surface of living a victorious, spirit-filled Christian life. They fail to handle the daily challenges of today's society. They never get started with developing, cultivating, and learning to enjoy a meaningful relationship with God. It is the most important decision of your life. Let's talk about it. The relationship starts with YOU.

Your relationship with God starts the moment you accept Jesus Christ as your Personal Savior and Lord. But, let's face it. Just like any human relationship, it must grow, be cultivated, and develop a quality of understanding, as you spend the time and energy to get to know one another. That's right! You and God need a serious, on-going relationship. An interaction that has a significant and important dialogue on a regular basis with lasting results.

Think about it. When you met the person who is currently your best friend, what did you do? How did that relationship become so meaningful and relevant to the extent that they know your favorite things? Well, I would guess that you spent quality time together, learning likes and dislikes, talking, laughing, and sometimes crying together. You went out to dinner with them, got to know each other, shared ideas, concerns, problems, and secrets. You both had mutual respect, a common bond, and an appreciation for the differences between the two of you that led to a genuine connection. And before long, it was obvious that you would become best friends. Well, the God of the Universe wants to have a deeper relationship with you and become your **real** best friend, for life. However, the choice is up to you.

Many will agree that God is love. And, that God loves everyone in the entire world. His desire is to have a healthy, meaningful relationship with you, to strengthen you, and make your life greater than you can ever imagine. But as a result of this wicked, hateful, world full of destruction and sin, He cannot look at you. God hates sin. We all know what sin is. That stuff you see, hear, and do that is contrary to the things you know are <u>right</u> to see, hear, and do. We actively participate and allow ourselves to be influenced by sin, negative people, and evil things that easily cross our daily path. In many cases, we succumb and refuse to turn our heads, and give in to the madness and chaos existing in our environment.

It is a known fact that sin separates us from a holy, righteous God who wants the best for our lives. He wants to be your best friend. No matter how much good we try to do, or how much better we try to live, nothing seems to work. The Bible says in Romans 3:23, "All have sinned and come short of the Glory of God." Rich, poor, young, old, male, female, and every ethnic group under the sun has fallen victim to the power of sin in this world. That includes rock stars, superstars, movie stars, and your favorite sports personality. They are also sinners in need of a personal relationship with God.

Therefore, because of His love for us, God sent His only begotten son Jesus Christ (John 3:16) to die on the cross in order to pay the penalty for the sin of the entire world. This was to redeem mankind or buy us back from the world of devils, demons, and destruction. By accepting Jesus Christ as the payment for your sin, you gain access to having a real, bona fide experience with God. Simply stated, Jesus is the only way to get back in right standing with God. The Word of God states in John 14:6, "Jesus saith unto him, I am the way, the truth, and the life, no man cometh unto the Father but by me."

In other words, good works, living right, taking care of loved ones, and all the other things we do to be good, perfect, and whole, won't get us an inch closer to acquiring and maintaining a relationship with God. Not only did Jesus die for your sins, but he was buried and after three days He rose from the dead, claiming all power in heaven and earth is in his hands as found in Matthew 28:18. And that, my friend, is called The Gospel (Good News) in common Christian circles— pure, plain, and simple.

So, the choice is yours. It's all in your ball court. You make the decision to personally receive Jesus Christ as your Lord and Savior. The Word of God in the Holy Bible describes the process of how that's done. You must confess with your mouth, and verbally ask out loud, and believe in your heart by faith that God raised Him from the dead (Romans 10:9-10). Then, you are saved, sanctified, and filled with the Holy Ghost.

Unfortunately, this is where many people fall off the map. At first, they go through the process of accepting Christ and join a local assembly of believers called a church. Or it's the other way around; they join a church, then accept Christ by praying the prayer of faith at some point later. And then the inevitable happens. Most get hooked into a "nice little church group," sometimes called an auxiliary or ministry or committee for a special program, and never spend adequate time to develop their newly found relationship with God.

The business and busyness of church groups, events, politics, programs, ministry directives, various religious conventions, retreats and so much more, generally prevent them from studying and growing in the Word of God. These overwhelming activities that are prevalent within a local church can prevent the necessary development of building a closer relationship with God. Therefore, the true transformation never really occurs and improvement lags behind in the lives of so many people who profess to "know" God. It emerges, but is not cultivated.

Instead, they live difficult, roller coaster, crisis-oriented lifestyles prone to constant agony and defeat. Their growth is stifled, hindered, and the joy promised and expected from the Word of God is not experienced. Living an abundant life as described in John 10:10, is a far-fetched idea. It doesn't manifest. In fact, it cannot be realized until the individual makes a real change with the decision and bold act to get started with Jesus. You can start over again, right now with confession and acceptance, and by turning the reality of your life circumstances over to God.

We have heard the term "time flies." And it is a true statement that no matter how much time you have, it never seems to be enough. And before you know it, a period, a year, or even a decade has gone by. We sometimes sit back and wonder, "Where did all those years go?" How did I get here so fast?

Life passes us by and we wonder about the goals that were set in the early stages of growing up. Quiet as it is kept, many people spend years, decades, even 30 or 40 years, *attending* church, and never really develop a personal relationship with God the Father, God the Son, and God the Holy Spirit. They usually wind up angry, bitter, sad, and disappointed with the Christian life. Some are prone to the interruption that comes from worldly standards and influences. This keeps them from growing stronger in Christ.

Instead, they usually settle for a mundane, tedious, unfulfilled religious experience as an average "churchgoer." The fullness of joy mentioned in Psalms 16:11 and John 16:24 is available, but not fully realized. Many Christians do not experience the "Joy of the

Lord," as mentioned in Nehemiah 8:10b. They just go through the motions—guessing, wondering, worrying, and remaining uncertain and anxious about their true status in Jesus Christ.

Rather than living the abundant life, they are snatched away by the enemy who is called the thief in John 10:10 and comes to steal, kill, and destroy. Such is the state of the person who has no knowledge or very little knowledge of the powerful impact of God's Word. They never really get started with understanding the importance of keeping a wholesome relationship with God. Fellowship with God is not clear and their daily walk with Him is limited to circumstances and issues surrounding their problems. But, Sunday after Sunday, you will find them heading out the front door, hitting the road, "to go to church." It becomes a weekly routine to give an hour or two to a holy, righteous God who has kept us safe throughout the previous week's assignments.

We meet, greet, eat, and say "goodbye" as we savor the joy for such a brief moment in time. We leave the premises talking about how good we feel, only to return to chaotic, harmful, discouraging environments, still unequipped to handle the daily opposition that we face Monday through Friday, and occasionally on Saturdays, when we go shopping. The Christian life becomes a monotonous, ordinary, routine, insignificant, frustrating, and painful experience as the individual struggles to survive.

The years go by with very little progress, significant change, or even minimal improvement because repetition becomes the mandate and we think that we are serving God. Frankly speaking, however, when we finally take an honest inventory, we realize that there is no spiritual growth with Jesus Christ, although we've been a "member" of the congregation, and sat on our favorite pew for many years attending church services, Sunday after Sunday. Where is the growth?

There **is a process** of Christian growth and development that is worth examining and putting forth to help you realize the importance of having and maintaining a victorious Christian lifestyle. In the book of 2 Peter 3:18, we are admonished, "But grow in grace and in the knowledge of our Lord and Savior, Jesus Christ. To him be glory both now and forever. Amen." With that goal in mind, let's get started with the **Process.**

Chapter 2

But Grow in Grace and Knowledge

GROWING SPIRITUALLY IS A decision that you make the moment you become a Christian. The time, energy, and commitment you give to it will dictate the level, meaning, depth, and strength of your relationship with God. Every good book starts with a great beginning, a strong middle section, and a wonderful ending. Some books are so good that the reader finishes with a sense of satisfaction from being entertained and educated to new heights. The Christian life is like following the script of a new book that takes your life to new opportunities, new horizons, and new experiences as you grow closer to God through Jesus Christ. You begin to see yourself and others very differently because your mind, heart, and soul become open to a better way of living in this world.

Imagine a pretty good life. Imagine a bad life. Imagine a mediocre life. As you ponder the path of these three entities, ask yourself, "Which one am I on? Where is my destiny heading? How good, bad, or indifferent are things going for me and my journey?" While you're thinking along those lines, let me share with you a wonderful verse from the Holy Bible that speaks to the matter. It's found in 1 Corinthians 2:9, "But as it is written, Eye hath not seen, nor ear heard, neither have entered into the heart of man, the things which God hath prepared for them that love him."

Wow, that is so amazing! In other words, you cannot even begin to imagine the wonderful life that has been prepared or set aside for those who genuinely love God. It's beyond our comprehension. The life that God has already prepared to give you is beyond anything you have ever seen or heard. In fact, our ability and comprehension to understand this great life is limited. We cannot see it with our own minds. It's not in the imagination of our hearts.

That statement written by the Apostle Paul tells of a life, not just well-lived, but a life incomparable, unknown, and unattributed to common, human understanding. This is a life reaching far beyond our basic desires and expectations. The life that God has prepared or set aside for those who love Him is "over the top." Then, why is it that so many Christians do not experience this abundant life? Many are bogged down with the same routine day in and day out which eventually leads to constant boredom, weariness, and a sense of worthlessness. We attempt to complete our tasks with minimal effort, only to find out that the void remains. We rarely re-group from the loss of dear loved ones to the harsh reality of physical death. And, failure seems evident, despite the energy spent to plan our goals.

A life without Jesus Christ can be a miserable experience of riding a roller coaster, where no matter how many times you jump into the seat, it always winds up to be the same old ride. However, there is a light at the end of the tunnel. It just depends on how long it takes for us to arrive at that location. As we read in the next verse,

1 Corinthians 2:10 says, "But God hath revealed them unto us by His Spirit; for the Spirit searcheth all things, yea, the deep things of God." This helps us to realize that the Holy Spirit reveals to us the things of God that He's prepared for us because the Spirit searches all things. Yes, the deep things of God. We receive the Holy Spirit once we accept Jesus Christ as our Lord and Savior. Therefore, the Spirit can teach us all about the things of God for this wonderful, Christian journey. We must yield ourselves and become available to learn about God. We all grow through a process. Let me share with you my personal journey.

My journey in Christianity started at age 10 going on 11, when "I joined the church." This led me to attend Sunday School regularly, and I started singing in the junior choir at a local Baptist church. By the time I was 15, I met my high school sweetheart. I considered myself a "good girl," because, for the most part, I was not doing what the "bad girls" were doing. I was the only daughter to my wonderful parents and had to keep my place in a house with four brothers. It took a while for me to grow out of being a "tomboy," but I finally made it. My mother would constantly remind me with her words, "You're a girl. You can't do things like the boys."

By the time I was 18 and about to finish high school, an older lady who sang in the Senior Choir at our church invited me to her home Bible Study. At that time, the Young Adult Choir called the Choraleers (ages 17 to 35) no longer existed and I was one of the few YOUNG people in the Senior choir, with all the older people! I loved singing praises unto God! We both sang in the soprano section of the choir. At the end of the week, I went to meet with the lady and she shared with me the importance of asking Jesus Christ to be my Lord and Savior. She asked if I had ever prayed the prayer of Salvation and verbalized the words, "Jesus come into my heart and be my Lord and Savior."

I told her about my experience in terms of walking down the aisle and shaking the Pastor's hand and saying, "Yes, I believe in Jesus," with tears rolling down my cheeks. But I answered her, "No, I never prayed a special prayer about this action." Mind you, by now I had been functioning in the church for approximately seven years and thought I was "good," and on my way to heaven (someday). From a personal viewpoint, I knew about sin and had my own personal sin to deal with, but my life wasn't challenged beyond the day-to-day concerns of being a bright, young lady, courting my high school sweetheart, getting good grades, and planning for college. Still, I knew that Jesus wasn't the *Lord* of my life.

I was pretty smart and cute, I was the only girl in the family, and I stayed out of trouble (for the most part) while believing in my own strength and control for my life. That was good enough. As long as I did the church thing once a week and kept my parents smiling, I was fine. However, this lady challenged me to move beyond the status quo and to grow beyond my own abilities, by asking the right questions about my real Christian walk with God. She told me to go into my own "secret closet" at home and pray to ask Jesus Christ to become my Lord and Savior.

What? I was so afraid, enlightened, ashamed, and glad all at the same time. You mean to tell me that I have been in this church all this time (1968 to 1975), singing in the choir, going to Sunday School, and attending services on Sunday mornings, and still may not be Saved, Sanctified and Filled with the Holy Ghost? What a rude awakening! The word HYPOCRITE came to my mind. Well,

I went home that evening and literally went into my bedroom closet and closed the door and prayed, "Lord Jesus, I need you. I thank you for dying on the cross for my sins, I ask you to come into my heart and be my Lord and Savior. Help me to repent and turn away from sin, and please Lord, make me the kind of person that you want me to be."

Tears began to roll down my face again, but this time I was sincere and wanted to grow in living for God. This woman started teaching me from a small study book called *Lessons on Assurance* by The Navigators. I used my Bible to answer the questions at the end of each lesson. Several weeks later (after some study time with her), I got baptized for the second time on the First Sunday at our church, making the public statement that I had really accepted Jesus Christ as my Lord and Savior.

Of course, many members in the congregation were surprised or astonished, but I stood my ground and held my head high, unashamed of the Gospel of Christ, for it is the power of God unto salvation to everyone that believeth, just like it says in Romans 1:16a. My mother and father were proud of me and really supported my actions. It was a re-dedication to The One who can make a difference in all of our lives, no matter what circumstances we face. And this time, our Pastor said, "Well, she knows what she's doing this time!"

Mind you, my Spiritual Mother had given him the heads-up on my decision to get baptized again, and profess my new identity with Jesus Christ. In fact, there were a few of us "young people" who made the decision to re-dedicate our lives by getting baptized a second time and making a deeper commitment to God. We were all grateful for her guidance, leadership, and encouragement at a significant time in our lives. Ironically, I sat under her tutelage for three consecutive years (1975 to 1978), which is the exact number of years that Jesus Christ taught the disciples before he died on the Cross for the sin of mankind.

So, from ages 18 to 58, I was blessed to have this wonderful, spiritually endowed woman who taught, shared, cared, and influenced my own Christian journey. She helped to train, encourage, and challenge me to grow during the hard areas of my life. She became my "Spiritual Mother," and I am grateful to God for sending her my way with wisdom and knowledge. She was allowed to cross my path just when I needed more of His grace and mercy.

So the concept for my book came to me in June of 2015 as I began to watch my Spiritual Mother die. Her health was failing and all medical attempts to improve her overall state were not working. I began to think about our relationship and the many lessons that God had afforded me from the individual and group Bible studies that she led in her home.

The interactions had a meaningful impact on my spiritual growth and development. I am a better person and have a better lifestyle as a result of the lessons that were designed to help me understand and navigate through my personal problems.

When I stop to reminisce about my "glory days" of going to college, getting married to my high school sweetheart, and relocating to New York City after he was accepted into New York Law School, I realize that we were a young, busy couple chasing our dreams for success. Then, after giving birth to our daughter, which by the way, occurred on the first day of law school, I soon started working (after six months) as a new supervisor in a community counseling program that was sponsored by a Jewish agency known as the Educational Alliance in lower Manhattan. We lived on Staten Island in a small, one-bedroom upper flat and caught the ferry to Manhattan every day.

Also, during this time, I decided to enroll in Graduate School at Rutgers University, which was located in New Brunswick, New Jersey (traveling by train), to work on my Doctorate Degree in Counseling Psychology. Although we had a lot on our plates, being the first college graduates in our families, we both knew that we could "make it." We had the desire and definite goals. We supported and loved one another. And we had the wherewithal to pursue our professional careers, despite the circumstances. It was an exciting, special time for both of us! We were very ambitious. Doing the impossible at all costs. Such a wonderful, magical time.

Yes, indeed! My Spiritual Mother was there for me—for us—as we faced the hard decisions and challenges that many young people avoid.

Over time, I would end up divorced and living as a single mother, moving back home to live with my parents, and operating a small business in a big city. Her wisdom encouraged me to stabilize my life, focus on raising our precious daughter, and find a way to regain my purpose. Our conversations and prayer sessions gave me: the bravery to handle the death of my beloved father in 1992 (I was a daddy's girl) and the shame from being deceived and cheated on by a church member; the ability to manage the care for my elderly mother; and the ability to work through my emotions/ feelings of devastation when she died in 2011.

After all that, I finally reached the stage of spiritual maturity to serve God in ministry, according to His Will for my life. When I summed up the scenarios, I thought, "Wow, what a blessing it has been having her in my world, every step of the way, training me, teaching me, letting me cry on her shoulder, and forcing me to grow throughout every situation for 40 years." I realize that it was her guidance and steady hand that enabled me to weather every storm that tried to drown my life, take my joy, and make me a neurotic mess! I can shout, "Thank you, Lord, for placing her in my life from 1975 through 2015."

She went to heaven to be with the Lord in February 2016. I am so grateful for her guidance in my life.

This prompted me to think in 2015 about the process of Spiritual Growth, which led to my Spiritual Behavior, which led to my Spiritual Maturity in many areas of my life as I learned to accept, thank God, and trust Him along the way. So, I told myself, "I need to document this process, the way it happened for me! I need to share this in a book or program at some point in time." Well, now is the time and I thank God that you are reading this material.

So, on June 21, 2018, the time was ripe and right for me to get started with the process, the book, the direction, and the lessons to help you and all Christians, who really want to get started with Jesus and grow in the Grace and Knowledge of our Lord and Savior as stated in 2 Peter 3:18.

The Process to get started with Jesus is real. There's no hocus pocus. God is not some genie in a jar where you make your wish and hope it comes true. He is the God of the Universe, the Creator of all things. God should be honored, respected, praised, and revered. He is holy and righteous. He is sovereign. His will is the authority for all of our lives. We were created by Him, for Him, to do His will on Earth as it is in Heaven.

The foundation of a viable Christian life starts with **The Holy Bible.** The **Word of God** is the only source for your daily bread. It was written more than 2000 years ago and it is the most profound book of the ages. The Holy Bible is the living Word of God that remains today, yesterday, and even tomorrow. In 2 Timothy 3:16-17, it states, "All scripture is given by inspiration of God and is profitable for doctrine, for reproof, for correction, for instruction in righteousness, that the man of God may be perfect (mature) thoroughly furnished unto all good works." It has been written in more than 300 languages. It penetrates the soul and gets to the heart of every matter known to mankind.

In Hebrews 4:12 it states, "For the word of God is quick (living), and powerful, and sharper than any two-edged sword, piercing even to the dividing asunder of soul and spirit, and the joints and marrow, and is a discerner of the thoughts and intents of the heart."

That is so powerful. The choices that we make and the actions we perform after Salvation lead us to a Christian walk of faith that continues to grow as we commit ourselves to the teachings in the Word of God. Generally speaking, we all start somewhere, at someplace in that special chapter in your own life that whispers, "Hey, you need God, Jesus, a Savior, some help!" It could be from job distress, death of a loved one, a divorce, a serious car accident, a health concern, children going astray, or a number of life issues that creep into our comfortable livelihood. Things do happen beyond our control that will draw our attention to God. You can read the same passage of scripture at different times in your life and get a deeper meaning or understanding depending upon the circumstances.

It's a known fact in the Christian community that it takes the power of the Holy Spirit to comprehend, interpret, and expound on the teachings of the Word of God. As we read in John 14:26, Jesus states, "But the Comforter, who is the Holy Ghost (Spirit), whom the Father will send in my name, he shall teach you all things, and bring all things to your remembrance, whatsoever I have said unto you."

You may wonder why so many people have said, "I read the Bible but I don't understand it. It doesn't make any sense to me. I can't figure out what it's saying to me." That is because it takes the mind of Christ to understand the things of God. The Bible states in John 4:24 that God is a Spirit and we must worship Him in spirit and truth. You should also read 2 Corinthians 2:12-14, which says, "And we have not received the spirit of the world, but the Spirit who is of God; that we might know the things that are freely given to us of God." There is just no human rationale for undertaking the Holy Bible and mastering its content. The Holy Scriptures are spiritually discerned providing interpretation, illumination, revelation, and enlightenment. When we read them, God is speaking directly to us. When we pray, we're speaking to Him.

Here's what happens. Basic Bible Beliefs AND principles of Godly living will manifest in your life as you take the necessary steps to learn the Word of God. When you begin to read, study, and meditate on the Holy Scriptures, the prompting of the Holy Spirit leads you to respond differently to life circumstances. There is an internal change, an urge, or nudge to live better and in more accordance with the principles of Godly living. For example, if you are a short-tempered individual, you begin to see yourself exercising more patience in your responses to people. You don't get mad so easily anymore. Rather than toss the used napkin on the floor, you actually find a nearby trash can to discard it. And even when you're driving, you change lanes more smoothly to avoid a potential crash from another discourteous, reckless, uncaring driver, rather than angrily pounding the horn in distress. I am sure you have had that experience!

We live in a society that, rather than encouraging people to seek and maintain the peace of God in their lives, we have accepted the term "Road Rage" and many drivers display that disgusting behavior. Such poor driving has caused deaths. However, the Word of God is so powerful and revealing that you begin to question the world's standard of living. Instead, you begin to ask yourself what God says about sex, love, homosexuality, sin, liars, death, time, hatred, marriage, money matters, dating, children, careers, sickness, and all the other problems that we face. Make the choice. Make up your mind. No more of this reckless, abandoned, crazy lifestyle the world offers. Decide to receive God's goodness from a deep, worthwhile study of His Way toward a better life.

The power of God by the aid of the Holy Spirit becomes more evident in your life as you study the Word of God. Take encouragement from 2 Timothy 2:15 which says, "Study to show thyself approved unto God, a workman that needeth not to be ashamed, rightly dividing the word of truth." So, we are admonished to study for our own knowledge and understanding without excuses for shameful, unrighteous living. As my mother used to say, "Get it for yourself." These areas commonly known to man are taken into consideration as you study from a biblical point of view versus the world's standards. You begin to question some of the decisions you have to make that are contrary to the Word of God.

As you begin to grow closer to God, you actually begin to like what Jesus Christ likes, say what Jesus says, do what Jesus did, act the way Jesus would act, go where Jesus went, feel like Jesus felt, and think like Jesus Christ in your day-to-day interactions. To sum it up, your walk in Christ becomes more evident as the Fruit of the Spirit is demonstrated through your new lifestyle in Christ. We find that in Galatians 5:22, where love, joy, peace, long-suffering, gentleness, goodness, faith, meekness, and self-control become a steady norm (internal compass) for your outward behavior. I have gotten to the place where I even pray before tackling a problem or entering a meeting where I am unfamiliar with the people and territory. I ask God to prepare me to speak, function as I should, and learn what is best for me in every situation. I have grown tremendously in this area of my life. It's better to not act hastily.

The Holy Spirit will also manifest in your life through consistent and regular study of the Word of God to lead you to hate what Jesus Christ hates. We know that God hates sin, liars, hypocrites, and everything else listed in Proverbs 6:16-19. This includes things such as a proud look, a lying tongue, hands that shed innocent blood, a heart that devises wicked imaginations, feet that are swift in running to mischief, a false witness that speaks lies, and whoever sows discord amongst believers. That is what God hates.

As you study the Holy Bible, you learn to memorize scriptures that become so important to "hiding" God's Word inside your heart. My Spiritual Mother would often encourage me to memorize certain verses for future protection. I didn't know what that meant at the time, but eventually when I was tempted or about to get into a "potentially sinful situation," ironically (by the power of the Holy Spirit), that particular Bible verse would come to my mind, and kept me out of harm's way. It's better to run with dignity than to act with pride! Trust me.

Psalms 119:9-11 is a great passage for hiding the Word of God in your heart (simply by memorization). It will keep you from living in a world of sin. Many stories from the Bible begin to take on new meaning and influence in your life. Things begin to make sense as you study diligently seeking direction, clarification, and understanding. The Holy Spirit is activated as you respond to the Word of God to teach and help you to remember, as stated earlier in John 14:26. It's sad to admit that so many people in the church today live in misery, under constant conviction and daily defeat, because they have not hidden (memorized) the Word of God in their heart.

I have heard on many occasions, "I have been in this church for over 20 years and didn't know that was in the Bible." Therefore, when trials come, temptation lingers, threats are evident, and tests emerge, they are not armed with God's protection and equipment to handle the battle. They are overtaken and flunk out. But the Word of God tells us to put on the whole armor of God so that we can stand in any situation. If we trust, believe, and follow directions, we can be strong in the Lord and in the power of His might, putting on the whole armor of God, as stated in Ephesians 6:10-11. The process never ends as long as we are living on Earth. We need to study the Word of God in order to experience and maintain a victorious, spirit-filled Christian life. The more we study and embrace the Word of God, the easier we can recognize evil, immorality, and wickedness in our society. We should take heed to 2 Peter 3:17b: "...beware lest ye also, being led away with the error of the wicked, fall from your own steadfastness."

So, by now, you might be wondering and have a number of

questions, so here are a few simple answers to help you along the way. How do you study the Bible? One day at a time. One subject at a time. One area at time. What do you need to study? Start where you believe you need the most help. I was 18 years old when I got serious and rededicated my life to God, so my Spiritual Mother started with the subject matter from Learning to Be a Christian Woman.

I had a study book, the Holy Bible, and my own current situation and its hang-ups. When do you study the Bible? As often as possible, daily, or weekly. Try to stay away from being a crisis-oriented Christian who only seeks God when the going gets rough. Where do you study? In a quiet place at home, or in a weekly Bible Study at a local church where you can grow spiritually. Who should lead you? A strong, faithful church leader, whose life and lifestyle demonstrate with evidence that they walk according to the Word of God. Pray for God's wisdom, direction, and influence in your search for a capable and available ministerial person. God already knows the true desires of your heart. And He will lead you in the right direction. As we grow spiritually, we must put the Word into operation. Yes, that's imperative. So here we go. **Lights, Camera, Action!**

Growing in Jesus

Chapter 3

His Way, Your Way, or The World's Way

It's one thing to know what the Word of God says, but it's another thing to actually do what the Bible mandates. This is where you really have to pull up your bootstraps and start walking "the walk." The journey is like the life of a long-distance runner. You are required to run the race with patience and endurance until you reach the finish line. As I recall my own path, you run the Christian race with diligence in the fear and admonition of the Lord. It is a life-long mission full of ups and downs, highs and lows, but the fullness of joy unspeakable is always present.

The secret key to living victoriously is to embrace the will of God for your life. That may be hard for most of us. That's because we think that **our way** is the best way. I remember the 1974 song by the late, legendary Frank Sinatra, "I Did It My Way." It was very popular, but talked about someone who walked through life with a proud stride, large and in charge of their own life, only surviving as best as they can.

We start out making our own plans without any kind of consultation, nor clear direction, listening to the voices of other people, trying to keep up with the Joneses, and moving about the Earth as if we know it all. Well, unfortunately, we don't know it all and before long, our life is a mess. We cry, get angry, have our regrets, and in many cases, attempt to blame God as if it were all His fault for our shenanigans and shambles.

But God loves us so much despite our faults. In the book of Romans 5:8, it states, "But God commendeth His love toward us in that, while we were yet sinners, Christ died for us." Through the death, burial, and resurrection of Jesus Christ, we now have access to a Holy God who desires the best for us. To become a doer of the Word and not just a hearer, as found in James 1:22, leads to a more effective outcome in our decision making. The challenges we face become less threatening because we are seeking answers from a stronger point of reference. As you study the Word of God, you begin to accept His will, way, and wisdom for your life, no matter the circumstances. This means to know His will, which is only found in His Word. It's not rocket science! You put into practice the mandates, principles, commands, and teachings of the Word of God. This step alone can lead to huge consequences. Before long, the principles will manifest in your life to help you solve your problems.

Where you once were bitter or depressed, the Word of God leads you to become pleasant and encouraged. For example, in Matthew 5:44, Jesus says, "But I say unto you, love your enemies, bless them that curse you, do good to them that hate you, and pray for them who despitefully use you, and persecute you." Now, that's a whole lot to swallow! Love my enemies? Oh, boy!

We know that the world says, *If you hurt me, then I am definitely going to hurt you.* We get bombarded from the nightly news reports of chaos, confusion, and conflict throughout our communities. But when I treat my enemies with love, kindness, smiling, offering help, and praying for them, I get better. I am better. They get better. And life is better. It becomes obvious that when you accept His will, you realize that it is the best option for your walk with Him.

In many instances, you may have walked alone, making decisions by yourself, or taking the advice from someone else who is just as miserable. That often leads us to run around in circles, not getting anywhere. In most cases, we tend to say, "I am my own person, I can handle this myself, or I'll do it my way." Well, you might have tried to do everything your way and still live in defeat. Let's get started with Jesus, move forward, and onward to a more excellent life, right now. I am convinced that God's way is so much better. I'll share some details, a little later.

The way of the world leads to discontentment and frustration. We are tossed and turned day after day. The problem with the world's way is that there are too many competing and conflicting voices. Everyone is trying to get your attention, take your money and ideas. Even lead you down a crooked path. There are millions of self-help books on various subjects. We have a host of get-rich-quick schemes on the market. Many directors and managers propose they have the key to progress, fame, and fortune. Unfortunately, the world is influenced by demonic and satanic forces of evil. Let me remind you that the devil is the prince of the power of the air, as mentioned in Ephesians 2:2. "And he walks about the Earth seeking whom he may devour," as stated in 1 Peter 5:8, like a roaring lion seeking his prey.

The Bible also teaches in 1 John 2:15-17 that the love of the world and the things in the world lead to destruction. For the lust of the flesh, lust of the eye, and the pride of life is of the world and not of God. And James 1:15 states that once lust has been conceived, it brings forth sin, and sin, when it is finished, brings forth death. But, as we put into action, and practice living the Word of God, accepting the Will of God, and growing in the Way of God, we are open to receiving His many blessings just waiting to be poured into our lives. This is stated in Ephesians 3:20: "Now unto him who is able to do exceedingly abundantly above all that we ask or think, according to the power that worketh in us." That is mind-blowing!

In other words, God actually ***waits on us*** to get it right or to get right with Him. He does not force Himself upon our own will. We have to be intentional (as my Pastor says) and want to have this dynamic relationship. There are many areas of human frustration in every classification of life. Your status does not make you exempt from problems and life crises. The rich, poor, young, old, working, unemployed, male, and female need help in this world. However, as you grow closer to Jesus Christ, you will begin to "see" examples of your growth evidenced in your Christian life. You will begin to move away from sinful habits, toxic relationships, mean-spirited individuals, self-centered folk, drama, bad situations, filthy communication, as well as inappropriate opportunities.

Your own personal growth will become more noticeable, obvious, intentional, and authentic in your relationship with Jesus Christ. You become more obedient to what the Holy Bible says when you hear the preached Word of God and you acquire a teachable spirit and attitude. This is so important. Your old way of doing stuff, taking matters into your own hands, and being in control, suddenly leaves. You begin to trust God, walk by faith, and believe in the power of His Word. You start to obey Him.

Let me give you a good example of how this works. We often "do stuff," and take matters into our own hands. The world tells you that it is "okay" to have sexual intercourse and to indulge in premarital physical interaction before you have said your wedding vows and have made the commitment to God and to each other. Following this road has led to many problems in modern society. This includes teenage pregnancy, physical illnesses, venereal disease, mental illness, abortions, psychological disorders, and social dysfunction, just to name a few. So many are suffering because they chose to believe in **the world's way**. My first job as a guidance counselor was to serve as a home health aide, working with pregnant teenagers!

Listening to **your way** can bring on more defeat and misery. When you tell yourself, "Well, I think he loves me, therefore it's okay," this creates another set of issues. These additional concerns may include low self-esteem, physical/mental abuse, sexual perversions, confusion, mind games, heartaches and pain, sickness, disappointment, promiscuity, depression, guilt, and shame. You'll wind up saying, "Lord if you get me out of this, I promise you that I will do **X**." Sadly, this usually becomes just another lie.

The Lord's way for sexual intercourse is present in Genesis 2:24, which involves, leaving, cleaving, and becoming one flesh. This verse describes the process of the marital bond according to the Will of God. It states, "Therefore shall a man leave his father and mother, and cleave unto his wife; and they shall become one flesh." Unfortunately, the teaching of this doctrine along with dating, courting, premarital interaction, male/female relationships, singleness, and inner youth conflicts are rarely discussed in our homes, schools, churches, and community circles. We simply don't make it a point until something happens. And by that time, someone has been hurt, abused, misunderstood, or victimized. Then we react! Sad to say, but true in so many cases.

I had to deal with this in my life as a young Christian woman. Although my high school sweetheart and I were planning to have a future together, we had already violated this principle in our dating patterns. When I brought it up, he agreed (not easily) that we should honor God's way of doing things and wait until we got married. After a considerable number of conversations, a few failed attempts, and some counseling about the possible repercussions, we made the constant effort to change while dating. We waited several months to consummate our love in marriage and had counseling during our engagement period. It was a hard choice, but we desired God's blessing and approval. The moral of this story is that I have learned that when you try God's way, He will help and deliver you. The verse that confirms this fact is James 4:8a, "Draw nigh to God, and he will draw nigh to you."

A common phrase in the Christian community is to "Let go and Let God." At first, I wanted to put more onto that expression and ask, "Let God do what?" But as I began to take the initiative to learn His way and what He was saying to me, my faith grew stronger. I learned to let go of everything that was weighing me down, hurting me, and keeping me from greatness and great things. I decided to let God handle it, let God fight my battles, and let God be in control of my destiny. In fact, Hebrews 12:1b says, "Let us lay aside every weight and the sin which doth so easily beset us, and let us run with patience the race that is set before us." I had to practice and believe that God knows, He cares, and He hears my every whisper. I can take refuge in Him, while I relax, and take it easy. He guides my path. I am safe and comforted. I am complete and whole.

When you choose to accept God's way, you will experience a new, refreshed and peaceful state of mind in your overall well-being. And all things, I mean all things, will become new as stated in 2 Corinthians 5:17, "Therefore if any man be in Christ, he is a new creature; old things are passed away; behold, all things are become new." You'll have a new walk, a new attitude, a new look, new vocabulary, new emotions, and yes (here's the big one) even new friends!

Finally, how do you practice? I thought you'd never ask. The way that you "practice" is by applying the Word of God to your personal issues that begin to surface. You "practice" by incorporating the Word of God into your regular habits, daily decisions, and actions. The Word of God becomes a conscious part of your normal routine. You "practice" by learning and memorizing scriptures. The Bible is no longer that book you carry on Sunday mornings when you go to church, or the book you pull out of the drawer when you're stressed out of your wits, or the book somewhere on the "back burner" of your life that your mother talked about.

The Holy Bible becomes the book of reason, acceptance, direction, guidance, truth, and necessity for understanding the Christian life. I love the way James 1:22-25 puts it plain and simple. We should be doers of the Word of God and not hearers only. And as we look into the perfect law of liberty and continue in it, we shall be truly blessed in our deed. Yes, the Holy Bible gives us the sacred ability to handle every struggle that we face in our humanity, right here and right now on earth. Welcome to God's Way. The only **real** way to handle every **Trial, Tribulation, Temptation, and Test.**

Chapter 4

Trials, Tribulations, Temptations, Tests

THIS MAY BE THE hardest chapter to digest. So, let's try to get through this one together. Unfortunately, the Christian life is not all foot-loose, fancy-free, keen, and wonderful. Well, at least not initially. In fact, it is not a bed of roses where everything in your life goes well. In some cases, there is a misconception that is perceived about this great, new life that comes after accepting Jesus Christ as your personal Lord and Savior. New believers are sometimes misled into thinking that all their burdens will soon be over, at the drop of a hat, and life is full of joy. Actually, it doesn't happen that fast!

But as we all know, the process of growing in anything takes time, energy, commitment, involvement, and a basic willingness to learn. Yet, I tried to be a quick study! Remember in an earlier chapter when I discussed how lost I felt after being in a church and not really being saved? Well, once I told my Spiritual Mother that I had prayed the "sinner's prayer," I quickly wanted to delve into all of the Biblical principles that I had not learned nor appropriated in my life. Not so! She tenderly explained to me that the process of growing closer to

God the Father, God the Son, and God the Holy Ghost, is a steady, gradual, process. It is demonstrated by the natural outpouring of His love for you and your desire to love Him. It is not wrapped up in a special formula that can be put into a box, manufactured, and then sold to the highest bidder! It's not done in your own strength. It takes the Holy Spirit who teaches and helps you to grow, learn, and do the will of God. Jesus speaks in John 14:26 and says, "But the Comforter, who is the Holy Spirit, whom the Father will send in my name, he shall teach you all things and bring all things to your remembrance, whatever I have said unto you."

There are genuine steps, and procedures that are taken. Christianity is not a rush job where you learn everything in one session, say "I got this," and then run off to Never Never Land, or some other wild country, preaching Jesus! It takes desire (your will), wherewithal, dedication, and yielding oneself to the instructions from God. There's one verse in the Bible that sums it up. It's found in 2 Timothy 3:16-17: "All scripture is given by inspiration of God, and is profitable for doctrine, for reproof, for correction, for instruction in righteousness, That the man of God may be perfect, thoroughly furnished unto all good works." In other words, the Word of God was inspired and given by God to Holy men (prophets) who wrote what is needed for us to have clear doctrine or principles, for reproving us when we do wrong, for correction when we sin, and for giving us instruction on how to live a righteous life according to Godly standards.

It is God's will that every Christian live a spiritually mature, perfect life exemplified by our good works. God anointed human beings to compose the Bible for us to know and obey His Word with confidence. It is stated in 2 Timothy 2:15: "Study to show thyself approved unto God, a workman that needeth not to be ashamed, rightly dividing the word of truth." The more we study, the more we learn, accept, and understand.

So, you see my friend, the Christian life is a journey of growing closer to God gradually as He helps you through your own personal trials, tribulations, temptations, and tests. It's unavoidable. You will experience some hardships when you join the family of Jesus Christ, and suffering is part of the process. It is explained in 1 Peter 4:1-2, 16, 19; that we identify with Christ when we suffer. And after the suffering, God will make you perfect (mature), stable, strong, and settle you as expressed in 1 Peter 5:10.

Immediately after you decide to start following God, all kinds of things begin to happen. It may appear like bad stuff is happening out of the clear blue sky. But actually, God begins to draw your attention to sin, the power of sin, and its controlling force. The negative consequences of sin that exist in your life become more obvious. This can be a painful experience because most of us think we're alright. We spend a lot of time comparing ourselves to others who are profoundly worse off, and we convince ourselves that we are in good shape. Well, the truth of the matter is that God knows the truth about you. He certainly knew the truth about me, no matter how well I hid my faults and sinful behavior. He dealt with the dark areas of my life, and I began to see myself through His lenses.

As soon as you put forth the effort to learn about God, there seems to be an invisible pull on your life to keep you living in darkness, feeling afraid, ashamed, and discontent. In some instances, you feel unable to break away from the course of evil that has dominated your life decisions. Even though you fervently seek God through prayer, studying the Holy Scriptures, and attending church services regularly, the weak areas of your life are subject to the beckoning call of sin. The Bible describes this picture in 1 John 2:15-17, as the lust of the flesh, the lust of the eyes, and the pride of life, which is not of the Father but is of the world. We also see this in Genesis 3:6, when Adam and Eve disobeyed God and ate the fruit in the Garden of Eden, which opened the door for sin to dominate the entire world. The power of one sinful act can destroy a lifetime of good intentions. Hey, that's mind-blowing!

You see, the Christian life, as beautiful as it can be, is filled with making the right decisions at the right time. Your mind and heart will tell you to "follow the way of Jesus Christ," but your body and feelings will tell you, "Okay... but not today." The Apostle Paul in Romans 7:15-25 described this contradictory pattern inside all of us and said we have to address it and turn it over to God. He starts by saying, "For that which I do I allow not; for what I would, that do I not; but what I hate, that do I." He goes on to explain the war in our members (body) against the war of our mind which brings us into the captivity of sin. It is only through Jesus Christ where we can win the war and overcome this internal battle.

That's why it is so important to confess your sins daily, repent, and turn away from the situations that have kept you in bondage. One verse that every Child of God should memorize is in 1 John 1:9, "If we confess our sins, He is faithful and just to forgive us our sins, and to cleanse us from all unrighteousness." We need to hide the Word of God in our hearts to keep us from being overthrown by the power of our sins.

Psalms 119:9-11 gives the formula for cleansing yourself to live a better Christian life. As we submit and take heed, the Word of God will keep us from wandering away from His commandments.

The Word will keep us away from the sins of this world. However, it needs to be hidden deep within our hearts (memorized). The Word is the lamp and light to guide your every step in the Christian life as expressed in Psalms 119:105.

You know how bad you felt when your parents told you to do something, and you told a big lie? Or how terrible it was when you treated someone wrong and didn't apologize, and later saw them at the grocery store? Do you remember how miserable you felt when you tried to do someone a favor, and it became a flop or an attack on your character? And, what about the time you chose to do the wrong thing, by turning your head? The issues we sometimes face **test** our faith and character. But God is our heavenly father who **chastises** us just as our earthly parents have done. He brings us to a peaceful state of righteousness as we learn to accept correction from authority as found in Hebrews 12: 6-11. We grow to revere God, just like we revere our parents, elders, government officials, the police, and those who are in positions of authority.

There is an example in the Holy Bible for every problem that human beings face. Along the way of growing stronger, there are many tests of our faith. The test of faith for Abraham occurs in Genesis 22:1-14 when God told him to take his son, Isaac up to a mountain to sacrifice him for a burnt offering. The obedience and faith of Abraham led him to stretch forth his hand to slay his son, but God called out to Abraham and stopped the motion. Instead, his fear of God (reverence) was demonstrated at that moment, and God showed him a ram caught in a bush to offer as the sacrifice. As a result, Abraham called the name of that place, Jehovah-ji-reh, which means, the Lord will provide.

Confession is the cure that leads to true forgiveness and repentance. **Temptation** is always lurking around and can be a vicious cycle. As you grow closer to God, you will become really sorry for the things you do against the will of God. For example, telling lies to get out of trouble, engaging in slick and deceptively clever behavior, showing the outright disrespect to others, and cursing every now and then. We can also include being prideful or angry about things you can't control, cheating (well?), stealing money, committing adultery, fornicating, hurting other peoples' feelings, participating in idolatry, and engaging in a long list of offenses that goes on and on. You never want to keep repeating the same old bad habits. If you do, you'll wind up living a defeated, carnal (fleshy) life as described in Romans 8:5-8, and cannot please God. Let me share a great example straight from the Holy Bible to illustrate my point. There was a man after God's own heart. His rise, fall, repentance, and restoration are a vivid description of God's grace and mercy.

The Bible records the story of King David, who started out as a shepherd boy. His life is a great example of someone who didn't appear to be important, but had a lot going for himself from God's viewpoint. It is recorded in 1 Samuel 16:7-18 that David was the youngest of the seven sons of Jesse who tended sheep. Ruddy and prudent, he was a skillful musician and a good fighter who had an agreeable attitude. The Bible says that God knew his heart and the Lord was with him. He was anointed, went on to do great things for God, had many victories, and became King over all of Israel, as found in 2 Samuel 5:3.

However, one day when he was off-duty from battle, he chose to sleep with another man's wife and she got pregnant! Then, he conjured a plan to set up the soldier-husband by encouraging him to sleep with his wife to cover up the pregnancy. But that plan did not work. So, he finally went to his last option and told his associates to make sure that the woman's husband was in the first flank of a battle so that he could be killed. And it happened! He did everything possible to *cover his sins*. Let me just pause right here so that you can breathe. Ready… inhale, exhale. Now, I will continue with his story. Because I want to help you understand how sin has this snowball effect on a person's life and gets bigger and bigger and bigger!

The Bible says in Proverbs 28:13 (written by David's son, Solomon), "He that covereth his sins shall not prosper, but whoso confesseth and forsaketh them shall have mercy." Shall have mercy! Shall have mercy!

So, King David, of course, thought that he was now off the hook, and could go on ruling with the attitude of "business as usual." However, eventually, he was confronted about his sins by the prophet Nathan (2 Samuel 12:1-12), which also led to some terrible consequences, and to his deep conviction and repentance. I encourage you to take time to read and study his life story. But the significant point I need to share about David is that he showed genuine remorse, sorrow, and disappointment for his sins. To grasp the intensity of his iniquity and transgression before God, he records his sorrow, his feelings, and desire to move from this horrible place.

His personal walk with God was disrupted and he wanted to be restored, as well as renewed by the power of God. In the precious **Psalm 51**, which is called a Psalm of Penitence, King David writes about his sin and desire to get back into right standing with God. He wanted to regain fellowship and communion with God. He wrote, "Have mercy upon me, wash me, cleanse me, purge me, and create in me a clean heart." His sincere desire was to be forgiven, renewed, restored, and upheld by God to go out and teach converting sinners to God's way of living. He craved to rejoice again. He wanted his life straightened out. And desired to sing praises to God, once again! After all, he was a great musician.

The growth pattern of the Christian life is one of peaks and valleys. It is a never-ending process of high and low moments. The **temptations** we confront and deal with are the things we enjoy doing that are contrary to the Word of God. That's why it is so important to know what the Word of God says, especially on the subjects that you find yourself wrestling with. But you don't reach a certain level and then graduate. You are always growing, getting better, becoming perfect (mature) in your spiritual life. I am still growing in certain areas of my life as I walk with God. The pattern for me has been to grow in the Word of God which leads me to change. Change occurs in my mind, patterns, attitude, outlook, habits, and perspective. Then my decision-making becomes wiser, more firm, certain, and in accordance with God's will. This in turn, now leads to richer outcomes, better consequences, and pleasant results where only painful reactions used to exist.

Another verse in 1 Corinthians 10:13 strongly suggests we can have power over any temptation. It's another good scripture to memorize. When you are tempted, God has made the way to escape! Believe it!

Here it is: "There hath no temptation taken you but such as is common to man; but God is faithful, who will not suffer (permit) you to be tempted above that ye are able, but will, with the temptation, also make a (the) way to escape, that ye may be able to bear it." You **can** get out of anything your sin has led you to do. There is an exit route, or pathway, a tunnel, and clear direction to reject the chance or opportunity to sin. As you remain free from that horrible lifestyle of captivity and bondage, you will shout "Hallelujah," with joy and enthusiasm knowing that you are accomplishing victory over sin.

One fact is for certain, and that has to do with your identification with Jesus Christ. Because you have changed from agreeing with the world's standards, you're not going to be liked by the children of darkness. There are many people in the world, and some are even weak, immature, carnal Christians who are still caught up in sin, worldliness, and evil pursuits. As Jesus Christ was lied on, persecuted, abused, and yes, even hated, you will be, too!

Jesus describes this behavior in John 15:18-20, and tells believers to expect to be hated by the world because the world hated Him. Not only will they hate you and Jesus, but they also hate God the Father (John 15:23). And in Matthew 5:11-12, Jesus tells us to rejoice and be exceedingly glad when we are persecuted for His sake and reminds us that the earlier prophets had that experience as well. When you read 2 Corinthians 12:9-10, the Apostle Paul reminds us that God's grace is sufficient for us. We can make it and take pleasure in all infirmities, reproaches, necessities, persecutions, and in distresses for Christ's sake. He says, "When I am weak, then I am strong" (2 Corinthians 12:10). The power of Christ rests upon us. He goes on to tell his young protégé, Timothy, that all who will live according to the way of Jesus Christ shall suffer persecution (2 Timothy 3:12).

Some people will try your faith, try your patience, and even speak ill of you. Jealousy, envy, and subtle competition will suddenly appear. I had my own **trials and tribulations** as a Christian and grew closer to God. My Spiritual Mother did not bombard me with a lot of "get ready for the doom and gloom" of the Christian walk. She didn't tell me about all this suffering and persecution, directly. But as I started to change my ways, the suffering began its course in my life, and I was forced to make the incredible decision to either follow in the discipleship training, or quit altogether and give up. You see, she was teaching me and all those who were in Bible Study with her, to be Disciples of Jesus Christ. I remember **my first big trial** occurred in **1976**, at age 19 as I began to study the Word of God consistently. Although attending college, I was also singing in a local female group which performed at night clubs. Saturday night sessions were often long and tedious. Even though I made it safely home after each performance, on many occasions I was tired in church the next morning, while singing in the choir.

I loved to sing gospel music and the words and lyrics often stirred my soul. Finally, one day I was given my first solo by the choir director and it became my mantra. I'll never forget the impact that "Don't Forget to Remember," by Tessie Hill, had on my life. I sang that song with so much fervor, energy, and authority. My mother wanted me to quit singing in the group at night, and as I think about it now, she must've been praying for me. One day she said, "Regina, I don't want you to be singing in those clubs."

"But Momma, I want to be a star!" I said.

Then she responded, "Well, why don't you be a star for Jesus." Ouch! I heard that cry (prayer) loud and clear. My heart was pricked and my mind started to wonder about that as a possibility? A few days went by and on the next Sunday morning, I got to sing my solo, "Don't Forget." This time, however, the power of the Holy Spirit filled me up and I felt like I was talking directly to God as I sang. I even added my own second verse/rendition to the song and I was overwhelmed. The members of the congregation were also affected, and I knew that God was calling me to a higher place in my relationship with Him. The next week, I went to the group rehearsal and quit! At that time, it was a huge decision, and a few years later, the group fizzled out. Several attempts failed to replace me and other members—who also changed their minds about a singing career in the entertainment industry.

Also, by now, my high school sweetheart and I were heavily courting and I told him we needed to quit having sex until marriage! **Another trial**, as any young lady who was in love, would agree. These weren't new principles, but they became re-ignited as I began to choose God's way over the decision to run my own life. My boyfriend and I struggled through the abrupt changes, but made them and eventually got married in **1978**.

I married the love of my life. We met on the bus in **1971**, while traveling home from Cass Technical High School, which was the best public school located in the city at that time. It was a special moment in the school's history because they were admitting the first new group of ninth graders in many years. Indeed!

The students selected to attend had good grades and came from different neighborhoods within the city. During our second year of high school, he asked me to be his girlfriend on Valentine's Day. When we started dating, it was such a magical moment. Somehow, I knew that he was the one! We had a lot of "firsts" and believed that we were made for each other. Our backgrounds were similar. We both had loving parents, similar religious values, active siblings, and a decent, wholesome upbringing. We were an ambitious couple, believing that the world was ours to conquer. And that is exactly what we set out to do! We designed a plan and began to execute it. It was so exciting and so much fun! Powerful!

Our marriage was a time of sharing, growing, caring, becoming friends, and learning a lot about life, its challenges, and what you do next when things start to go awry. It's funny when I think about it now; we had built our lives centered around each other so much, that when the break-up was really happening, we couldn't believe it was really happening. The marriage consisted of getting busy to have a "good life," by educating ourselves, starting our careers, making some money, and mapping out our goals together. The quest was to follow our dreams and to live them. We were always together.

Unfortunately, we forgot about the importance of regularly attending church, maintaining fellowship with believers, and getting some help when those problems emerged beyond our control. It **was on** the back burner. In addition, our eyes were not focused on the seduction that began to attack our marriage, and overtly steal the wonderful outcome of our hard labor. The goal of enjoying the benefits of a successful lifestyle quickly slipped away. And we wound up getting a divorce. This was strange because I was used to a structured family with love.

When you get too busy, you can easily get distracted and start moving in a direction that causes a downward spiral. Different directions (between a husband and wife) can lead to weird distractions, defeat, disappointment, destructive behavior, depression, and outright disbelief. We had done so much together that functioning apart from one another, at first, was a mess.

Our only child was born on the first day of law school in 1980. I was hoping for a boy and did not expect to have a bouncing baby girl. So, when she was born, he had her name all spelled out, by taking our two names and putting them together. She became his pride and joy. We agreed to always exceed the expectations and make sure that our daughter had the best life possible. We realized that she was not the problem and did not deserve to get trapped within our marital issues.

Despite the drama, he became a great criminal attorney, and I became a great guidance counselor. Our daughter, a classical music major, opera singer, and college professor, is a blessing and has brought us so much joy. To my surprise, in **1986** after the divorce, the Lord allowed me to "stumble," into a small business venture which has served thousands of consumers for 35 years. This gave me a new life, a new dream, and a new direction. God is so good. You must learn to trust Him.

So, you see, **life goes on** and you can set your goals and objectives, but bad things do happen to good people all the time, and especially when you embark upon the journey of living the Christian life. Satan is lurking around constantly as recorded in 1 Peter 5:8, just waiting to devour and take you out!

Another strange thing happened which I consider being a **trial.** On one Sunday morning, when the music played, another soloist in the alto section was given the microphone and chosen to lead "my song," which is called, "Don't Forget." (I will never forget this incident!) She did a fine job, but it was not "me" singing as I had done previously on several occasions. I was hurt to the core and very disappointed, but my Spiritual Mother told me to keep pressing on for Christ. It was several years later before I got the chance to sing that solo again. But God is faithful, so I stayed in the choir and continued to walk by faith, trusting that he would deal with the jealousy and the conflict, and rescue me from envious people, yes, church people.

I listened to my Spiritual Mother, who reminded me that my labor and service to God were not in vain. The scripture says in 1 Corinthians 15:58, "Be steadfast, unmovable, always abounding in the work of the Lord, forasmuch as ye know that your labor is not in vain in the Lord." And she encouraged me to keep pressing toward the mark for the prize of the high calling of God in Christ Jesus, as the Apostle Paul so eloquently puts it in Philippians 3:14. Trials may come and go, but you have to keep trusting and believing that God will work it out. He always has a better way of handling conflict and will work it out for your good as found in Romans 8:28, and here is what it says, "And we know that all things work together for good to them that love God, to them who are the called according to His purpose."

But **life goes on** and your determination to rely on God can go from experiencing trials to tribulations. When my husband was in law school, I learned that a trial is the examination of the facts of a case before a court of law. It involves hearing the evidence, witnesses, presenting each side of the case, and deciding on a person's guilt or innocence. As a Christian, many trials are accompanied by suffering and affliction. Sin is usually the culprit. Someone or some group ends up being the victim.

Tribulations are extended trials, where you are tested, tempted, tried, found guilty, and then you repent and move to this higher plane of existence in your personal walk with God. They are severe, harsh, and extreme. It is a different experience for every Christian. I believe that for those who are sincere, God puts "His mark on you." Tribulations can last for days, for months, and years. They make you stronger and bolder, and you wind up with a zest and zeal to serve God in a more substantial way. Your commitment reaches a higher level as you serve God. There is an explosiveness that emerges from your total being as demonstrated by your extended growth in faith, joy, love, and the peace of God. You become an obedient, active, doer of the Word of God, once you **get to the other side of a tribulation.** You are intense, intentional, and intending to make a difference in the life of another lost soul, disappointed individual, or lonely person.

How do I know? Because no matter how bad it gets, God will deliver you and take you to the other side. I am thankful to God that **I made it** to the other side. And He gave me a special verse, Psalms 40:1-3. Let me share it with you. It says:

> I waited patiently for the Lord, and He inclined unto me and heard my cry. He brought me up also out of a horrible pit, out of the miry clay, and set my feet upon a rock, and established my goings. And he hath put a new song in my mouth, even praise unto our God; many shall see it, and fear, and shall trust in the Lord. (Psalms 40:1-3)

After the divorce in **1986,** while raising my daughter and coping with the death of my father which occurred in **1992,** I made the decision to get more involved at church. My father was a faithful member of the Usher Board and I wanted to serve in a greater capacity to continue his legacy. I needed to do something beyond just singing in the choir. I knew quite a lot about the Bible from my studies and lessons. I also had experience in dealing with some real problems. So, in **1993,** I joined the Board of Christian Education at my local church, under the leadership of my very first Sunday school teacher who taught me when I first "joined the church" at 10 years old.

She started training me in that ministry for leadership. I shared with her my desire to establish a Christian Counseling Program. She was very kind, open, and quite informative. An Associate Minister and his wife recommended that I team-teach along with a wonderful spirit-filled couple who were in charge of the young adult Sunday school class. They welcomed me and my daughter with open arms. They also had two daughters of their own. We grew closer in fellowship and friendship. I really enjoyed teaching and felt that I was beginning to contribute more to ministry, given what I had learned along the way.

However, quiet as it is kept, my biggest hurt and devastation in that church was about to occur. It really threw me for a loop! Sin, surprise, and a sad situation!

One Sunday, I was approached by a gentleman who came to the choir stand as I was about to leave and he asked for my telephone number. By this time in my life, I had been divorced for several years and was hoping to get involved in a healthy, Christian relationship. I specifically recall suggesting to him that we keep the interaction "quiet" because if things didn't work out between us, I did not want to get into a mess from dating another church member. In all my years, I had never dated anyone at that church. However, dating this gentleman led to several months of dating, sex, some nice dinners, and a few interactions that included our kids. He also was a divorcé and had a son. Suddenly, he started to slow down the contact and make excuses, as if he were trying to move in another direction. I was baffled, but just started praying harder, asking God questions, and hoping for the best answer. I prayed, "Lord please **reveal to me** what is going with him in this relationship?" Well, God certainly gave me the answer, freed me, and said, "You're still my child."

One Sunday, the announcement clerk was pleased to announce the upcoming wedding of that gentleman and his soon-to-be bride! They stood up together, and everyone in the church clapped. I, on the other hand, was shocked! Immediately after that, the choir director played an up-tempo song where I led as the soloist.

I will never, ever forget this moment! Forgive? Yes. Forget? No. You ask why? Because God allowed this **significant critical event (SCE, a counseling term)**, to happen in my life, in order to bring me into total subjection to His will and authority. I learned that God wanted me to serve Him with my whole heart. He wanted me to be totally committed to my Christian life. To walk right, talk right, act right, and live right. To love Him with my whole heart. This is the first and greatest commandment. It is found in Matthew 22: 37-38, "Thou shalt love the Lord, thy God, with all thy heart, and with all thy soul, and with all thy mind."

As I finished the solo and began to walk back to my seat in the choir stand, I turned back around, walked to the microphone, and quoted Romans 1:16-17.

And I blurted out, quoting Romans 1:16: "For I am not ashamed of the gospel of Christ; for it is the power of God unto salvation to everyone that believeth; to the Jew first, and also to the Greek." And I continued by saying, "This man who is planning a wedding, had dinner with me last night, and now this? Satan is destroying a lot of people's lives."

Then I started crying, and immediately a few women who were Deaconesses rushed me into a quiet room. They asked what was wrong with me? What was the matter? Why did I do that? I simply told them the truth and said, "He was out with me last night; he never told me that he was going to announce this wedding to another woman! We've been dating for several months! He never told me!"

They were not really empathetic, so I went home. The first person that I called was our first lady and I told her what I had done at church. She had stayed home on that particular Sunday. Then I called my Spiritual Mother, and she gave me some comforting words of wisdom. My only consolation was that my dear 66-year-old mother and 13-year-old daughter were not in service on that Sunday morning. Thank God! But I felt awful. And it was ugly. I was furious! I had been seduced, mishandled, rejected, and made to be a fool, at the same time, in a church where I attended regularly, served faithfully, and loved God.

But as I stated earlier, **life does go on.** It does get better. Time passes, things change, and you begin to heal. God is a deliverer, a shelter, and a strong tower to help in the time of need (Psalms 61:1-4; Proverbs 18:10).

The following Sunday, I was approached by the wife of the Associate Minister (the ones who had recommended me to team-teach) and she told me to keep coming to church, despite my feelings. She encouraged me to keep on serving God. I would make it through this dramatic situation.

The time went on and I had a few counseling sessions with the Senior Pastor of the church. I stayed with my facts, even though the staring, glaring, and whispering were evident. However, that gentleman was placed on probation for a year, given that he was an officer of the church. The couple went on living and consummated their love in marriage. Meanwhile, I decided to pull away from my teaching responsibilities, and seek God for true repentance, forgiveness, and to regroup. I continued to participate in the Board of Christian

Education and remained in the choir, but I did not teach. My teaching partners understood my decision and prayed for me. And, **life goes on**, but another twist was waiting for me around the corner.

By **2004**, my mother was growing old and needing regular attention. My brothers were complaining and blamed me for everything, which caused a lot of family disputes. Something said in a still, small voice, "Why don't you go back to Sunday school?" I realized that the Holy Spirit was guiding my life back to the Word of God to seek answers for our household and family problems. The teacher was dynamic and I began to grow in my areas of weakness and prayed consistently, about my family issues. Things began to improve in my life, and I felt better about my walk with the Lord. I made an active decision to avoid conflict and heated discussions by guarding my heart and tongue. Time has a way of healing all wounds, and patience seems to be its healthy companion.

After two years passed, I was asked in **2006** to join the Women's Day pulpit committee, which was spearheaded by the first lady of the church. It was a great opportunity to acclimate myself to the program logistics of the church. Next in **2009**, there was a need for someone to teach in the New Members Ministry.

I volunteered to teach that class which focused on helping new Christians learn basic principles on spiritual growth. It was a blessing to see and experience the joy that new converts express, as well as witness the change in new members.

Finally, before our long-term pastor died in 2014, I became the Chairperson for a great fundraising effort to generate money for the future well-being of the church, and we successfully raised $30,000 from **2009 to 2011**. Looking back, I now realize that my tribulation in that church lasted for 15 years.

What else can I say about **trials, tribulations, tests, and temptations?** What is the real take-away? Well, I am inclined to agree with James 1:2-4, which says, "My brethren, count it all joy when ye fall into various trials (divers temptations/KJV), Knowing this, that the testing of your faith worketh patience. But let patience have her perfect work, that ye may be perfect and entire, lacking nothing." I am now mature, more patient, and living victoriously.

God has been so good to me. His grace and mercy have sustained and kept me every step of the way. He has taught me to stand on His promises that have manifested in my life. He has blessed me and continues to look after me. I am sharing this writing with you because of His Magnificent Power to understand, heal, strengthen, and deliver. God is real.

And quite frankly, **I have decided to Stay With Jesus.** He is the Way.

I thank the Lord daily, for the fruit of the Holy Spirit, as mentioned in Galatians 5:22: love, joy, peace, longsuffering, gentleness, goodness, meekness, faith, and temperance (self-control), which keeps me fervent in spirit. I am forever grateful for His love, redemption, and protection.

Photo Gallery
Section 1

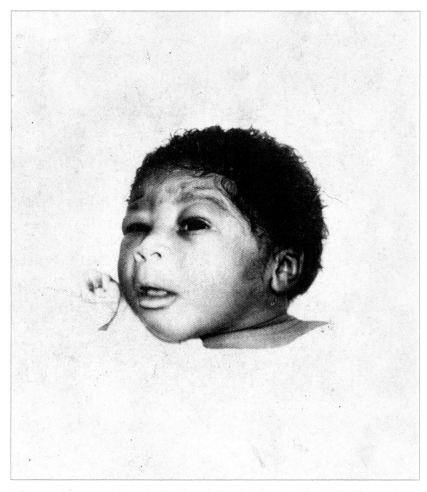

After two boys came into the family, a baby girl, **Regina Alexis Hinkle**, was born October 19, 1957 at 3:44 p.m. at Women's Hospital in Detroit, Michigan.

When I was two years old, my brothers, Junior and Ronnie, looked after me while playing in the backyard.

Here we are: Samuel, Jr., me, Dwayne, and Ronnie in our living room with that famous black and white television from the 1960's.

Learning at Camp when I was 10 years old was fun, thanks to my cousin Vernice who was a Group Leader.

My 7th grade graduation profile, as I left **Hanneman Elementary** to attend **Munger Jr. High School in 1970.**

My loving parents, **Mr. and Mrs. Samuel Matthew and Rosie Lee Hinkle**, were affectionately known as "Sam and Rose." They were a happy couple who taught us to believe in God, goodness, giving, and gratitude.

Our family in 1966 with Mom: Samuel, Jr., Ronnie, me, William (Dwayne), and Jimmy. Dad was the photographer.

My brother, **James Allen Hinkle (Jimmy)**, received an award from the **City of Detroit in 1979,** presented by **Councilman Nicholas Hood, II.** My parents were also present.

My dear **"Auntea"** (Mary Ethel) and Uncle Sylvester Freeman are with **Alexis Jane (I'm her namesake)** and her baby, Janice Michelle.

Aunt Nancy and Uncle George Manuel taught me their style of bowling and always gave me a kind gift whenever they would visit Detroit. I admired them.

I never met my beautiful Aunt Harrietta Hinkle (Cousin Jr. Ruffin's mom); but heard many stories about her life when I was growing up.

My mother's brother, **Uncle Robert Lee Creag** who was so much fun, lived with us (1973-1982) after his service in the US Army.

Our cousins from Chicago, Illinois often visited during childhood. Dwayne, Bernard, Catherine and Lindsey Cooper (twins), and I loved playing outside.

Aunt Mary Ethel Freeman and Uncle Harry Hinkle share a pleasant moment on his birthday when he was in Detroit, MI.

I traveled with my parents to visit my great Aunt Mary and Uncle Samuel Neal who lived in Springfield, Ohio.

My first cousins, **Helen Hinkle** (Uncle Harry's daughter), and **Louis Ruffin Jr.** (Aunt Harrietta's son); were inspiring role models who motivated me to follow my dreams.

Staying with Jesus

Chapter 5

Stay the Course, No What Matter

NOW THAT YOU KNOW how to Get Started with Jesus and grow in your relationship with Him, some questions will come to mind. Such as, is it worthwhile to stay in this relationship? Am I gaining any significant results that have made a tangible difference in my life? What is really happening here?

Your commitment to stay with Jesus is going to be challenged as soon as you make up your mind to follow God. Once you accept His methods for improving your life, you'll be attacked subtly and overtly by the enemy. The devil (Satan) has one goal in mind, and that is to pull you back into a world of sin. He wants to discourage you and will tell you that your old way of living was fine. So, get ready, and be on the alert! We are told in 1 Peter 5:8 to be sober, be vigilant, because your adversary, "the devil, as a roaring lion walketh about, seeking whom he may devour." These actions of Satan are vividly described in Job 1:6-7. Jesus Christ even says in Matthew 26:41: "Watch and pray that ye enter not into temptation: the spirit indeed is willing, but the flesh is weak."

That is no joke! The devil is so angry that you have chosen Jesus Christ, that even your old friends and buddies will disagree with you and say you're on the wrong track. Some people may try to pull you into unproductive conversations, and religious rhetoric, in their attempt to force you to prove what little you know.

Staying in your relationship with Jesus Christ is a decision that you alone have to make. It is your choice. God does not force His way into our lives. You have to come into the realization that it is worthwhile, and in your best interest to stay the course and run (hang out, fellowship, participate) with Jesus Christ. Challenges become real and they are a rude awakening as to how far off the mark you really are in our walk with God. Discouraging situations seem easy and at times unstoppable. Old habits tend to haunt you or linger. And those friends who meant you harm, suddenly re-emerge at the forefront of your mind. We sang a song in Junior Choir, "I have decided to Follow Jesus." Once you're on this journey, you will *say and sing,* "I have decided to Stay with Jesus," no turning back.

Because whatever you are facing, or going through, this **too** will pass. There is hope, that blessed hope in Jesus who has redeemed us, as given in Titus 2:13-14.

One of my favorite passages in the Holy Bible is mentioned several times throughout various stories and events: **"And it came to pass."** This phrase usually indicates a dynamic, dramatic shift, or change from a lesser meaning to a greater, better outlook or point of view. It implies that whatever was wrong got better, or some negative issue became a positive manifestation. For example, the fascinating story is told about the trials and tribulations that Joseph experienced in Genesis 37-48. He was a dreamer, the youngest son of Jacob, and his older brothers didn't like him. He was thrown into a pit, then sold, and carried off to Egypt.

Joseph wound up living in Potiphar's house, an officer/captain of Pharaoh. He was falsely accused of sleeping with Potiphar's wife in Genesis 39. There, the phrase, "And it came to pass," is recorded eight times, detailing the sequence of events leading up to the accusation and punishment (Joseph was thrown into prison). However, the scripture also records in Genesis 39:21, that the Lord was with Joseph, showed him mercy, and gave him favor during prison. He went on to become a great leader in Egypt and saved his entire family from a devastating famine. Joseph stayed with God, no matter the consequences.

You see, as the process unfolds before your own eyes, it becomes more and more real to you. When the results come in from answered prayers, extended blessings, and a better understanding of mankind, your relationship with Jesus Christ becomes meaningful. As you begin to experience some of the benefits and privileges from your own obedience, you'll make the right decision to not let **anything** destroy your sense of progress in the Lord. As your faith increases— "For we walk by faith and not by sight," (2 Corinthians 5:7)—you become aware and sensitive to the satanic attacks on your life. You are ready to defend yourself against past sins and able to confront behavior that can lead to evil pursuits.

Think about it. Most of our sin doesn't creep up on us. We usually make an active decision to participate in sinful behavior. However, as you count the costs and examine your own life with Jesus Christ, you must decide if Jesus Christ is better than all of the rest, or the previous things that have been thrown into your face over the years. Take a moment right now to ask yourself and examine where your life was headed before your relationship with Jesus Christ began, and determine if the journey (however long) thus far is worth continuing.

Many human relationships start out fine, yet they often wind up causing so much heartache and headache, along with emotional and physical pain. A concrete evaluation of your own personal progress can help you make the best decision. Psalms 119:9-11 can help you evaluate your relationship with Jesus Christ. Our ways become clearer as we soak our minds with the Word of God. Taking heed means to listen on purpose, intentionally, paying careful attention to God's instructions and His messages. Then, carefully and consistently hide His Word into our hearts through the process of memorizing the Holy Scriptures.

As you ponder and take the necessary time to examine your worthwhile experience with Jesus Christ, don't let anything or any person hinder your process. Don't allow anyone to change your mind about your own experience with Jesus Christ. The plan God has for you is not the plan God has for me, or him, or her, or them. We all have our own measure of faith and gifts, distributed exclusively by the Holy Spirit as found in Romans 12:3-8 and 1 Corinthians 12:4-11. As members of the body of Christ, we each have an assignment, a responsibility, a task, and spiritual gifts to help build up the Kingdom of God. Many distractions and detours will attempt to grab hold of your attention to change your focus. But you must stay the course. Don't drop out. Stay away from sin, Satan, situations, and seductive people who mean you harm, while promoting their agenda and negative influence in your life.

As you stay the course in your relationship with Jesus Christ, you will develop and mature in the Word of God, and the sweet communion of the Holy Spirit will bring the proper scriptures to your mind to aid you during tough times. The Holy Spirit will help you discover a greater purpose for your life. The Holy Spirit will specifically point out bad behavior and help you discern good and evil. He is the great Comforter who lives inside you and will never leave you, as stated in John 14:15-21. He is your "internal compass" to lead and guide you.

Spiritual maturity is the goal as you gain hope, strength, and relief from past mistakes and years of "living in the world." You will find yourself growing like a newborn baby, from the "milk of the Word" to the meat of the Holy Scriptures. Milk is for babies. Meat is for fully grown individuals. In the Christian life, we go from strength to strength, learning the principles that are easy to accept, as well as the principles that reveal and convict us of sin. This is mentioned in Psalms 84:5-11, 1 Peter 2:2, 1 Corinthians 3:2, and in Hebrews 5:12-14. As you stay the course, you will find your appetite changing from "worldly food" to "spiritual food." Your taste buds are no longer sour and stale, but present a sweet, savoring palate. And you'll find yourself smiling more often. Then you'll come to understand and appreciate that joyful, verbal expression that many Christians shout, "God is good, all the time, God is good!" Oh, yes He is!

It is so important to rehearse over and over, again asking yourself: What was my life like before I accepted Jesus Christ and this new journey? Can you remember? Review what you were dealing with and the situations that you were trying to handle, alone. Maybe you were like me. Taking too many chances? Trying to figure out your life circumstances? Constantly experiencing frustration due to another bad decision? I encourage you right now. Take a minute to reflect upon what He did on Calvary and why that is important for mankind and you. It is so refreshing to do a **Before Christ** and **After Christ** synopsis of your own life, as you search for the peace of God which comes from walking with Jesus Christ. He died, was buried, and on the third day, "early one Sunday morning," rose to set you free. You can now claim victory over every situation and eternal life. Hallelujah! Thank you, Jesus! Praise the Lord!

Remember this first simple equation: God–Jesus Christ–Mankind. Jesus Christ brings sinful mankind back to our holy, righteous God. By His death on the cross, burial, and resurrection, He bridges the gap and separation which is caused by sin. And remember this second equation as well: God–Christ–Mankind–Holy Spirit. Jesus sent the Comforter to help us in times of trouble and to follow his example. The Holy Spirit intercedes on our behalf (Romans 8:26-27), helping to keep us connected to God the Father. The Comforter lives inside of you and gives us the power to teach others, lead the way, and follow the directives given by Jesus Christ. He specifically told His disciples (followers, believers), to go, teach, and baptize all nations (everyone) in the Name of the Father, Son, and Holy Ghost as found in Matthew 28:18-20. We call that, "The Great Commission." We are supposed to teach everyone, to observe all of the things that Jesus Christ has commanded and the things He did when He walked on Earth. He promises to always be with us wherever we go in this whole, wide world. Jesus never fails. He is with you until the end of your battle, the end of your troubles and problems, your circumstances, issues, concerns, and until the end of your life.

As I reflect on my personal journey, I have come to realize that the Christian life is not a bunch of dos and don'ts. It's more like, "Is this better or the best way to live my life? Is it worthwhile?" Your relationship with Jesus Christ must mean something to you. Does it mean anything which can lead to more positive results in my life? My answer is a resounding "Yes." Yes, definitely. It is so beneficial and rewarding. I wouldn't have it any other way!

Looking back on my own spiritual growth and development in my personal relationship with Jesus Christ, I did not have a road map. I did not have a set program to follow. Yes, there were some books to guide me and Christian workbooks to help me along the way. But most of the Christian journey is a step, a walk, a run in a slow, steady, gradual race of faith as mentioned in Ecclesiastes 9:11, Romans 1:16-17, and Hebrews 12:1-2. On a personal note, this concept of walking by faith is really a great mystery of God as recorded in 1 Timothy 3:16 and 2 Corinthians 5:7. It's funny, because you don't know how you're going to get to the other side to experience a better way, a better life, or a better situation. But deep down inside, you believe and know that it is there, just waiting for you to cross over, get there, to receive it, and experience it. There is blessed hope in the Word of God! This hope is stated in Jeremiah 29:11, 1 Peter 5:10, 1 Thessalonians 1:3, and Colossians 1:23-27.

But I specifically recall some of the literature that was used to foster my spiritual growth. I list the names of some of the books in the bibliography section of this writing. There were Christian events and retreats sponsored by different organizations. I loved my Spiritual Mother's approach in motivating us to go in groups to "do the work of the Lord." We went out to witness in various settings, attend religious seminars and visit other churches. One summer we traveled to a Christian Festival in another state, and I also remember going to a women's retreat that was held at a college campus.

It was so much fun as we learned about Jesus, and how to improve our lives as young people. We were on a mission and believed that it could be accomplished.

She was so keen and astute in seeking the appropriate Christian material, along with the Holy Scriptures, that correlated to the specific problem area that was staring me in the face. It was a known fact that she genuinely cared about all of her students. She had a biblical library, full of material that was utilized to help all of her students grow in the areas where they needed the most help. She would find the correct information. Her style of teaching was unique, open-ended, practical, and challenging, while her discussions were extremely beneficial.

In the Holy Bible, there are many stories, examples, and answers to the thousands of problems that we face from generation to generation. This is so amazing and fascinating to me. I am in awe when I read a passage of scripture that speaks directly to my concern, for that specific moment in time. And, to top that off, it might be the same scripture that I read several years ago, of course, at a different stage in my life. I love this particular verse in Hebrews 4:12, which says, "For the word of God is quick (living), and powerful, and sharper than any two-edged sword, piercing even to the dividing asunder of soul and spirit, and of the joints and marrow, and is a discerner of the thoughts and intents of the heart." My response to that verse is "Wow!" The word of God is so P-O-W-E-R-F-U-L!!

Over the years, I have learned that our problems (sin) fall into three major categories: sex, money, and communication (discussed in marital counseling). So, at various stages of my life as a Christian woman, I have been challenged to confront, admit, deal with, and reconcile my own behavior in different scenarios. When I finally stopped comparing myself to others and placed my interest in letting Jesus be **the Lord of my life**, things changed for the better. My plate was no longer full. I became more available to serve God with my whole heart. And living according to His standards became a priority.

So, you see, God had to shake me up and allow my feathers to get ruffled, which turned my life around. I grew from being an average, every day, ho-hum, carnal Christian to a Spirit-filled Christian Woman, leaning and depending on God for peace and joy. I began to take my relationship with Christ seriously. He's more than a Sunday morning routine. Yes, there were some heartaches and pains along the way. But victory and deliverance have been so precious. I am truly blessed in my personal journey with Jesus Christ, my Lord, and Savior.

Now, I am thankful for His grace and mercy, which helped me to change and move from not trusting His way, to accepting and believing in His will as the best option for my life. I got better, made mistakes, recovered, asked a lot of questions, changed my mind, went back to God, cried a lot, and said I'm sorry. Ultimately, the process of growing and maturing to a better place in life is very real and dynamic. However, it takes time. It takes a willingness on your part; it takes desire, it takes things happening to get your attention which draw you closer to Him. It takes correction, reproofs, doctrine, making the decision to get it right; it takes long discussions, some disappointments, confession and repentance. I did my share of crying, and starting over, and starting over again, but growing stronger, and more determined to be dedicated to His instructions (2 Timothy 3:16-17). His directions are clear and concise, especially when we follow them.

As I shared in Chapter 3, most of all it takes a sincere desire to study the Word of God as 2 Timothy 2:15 commands, and saying

"No," to "My Way," (that famous Frank Sinatra song of the 1970s), and "Yes," to God's Way.

You need a base to operate from, such as a good, Bible-believing church, where the Word of God is preached, taught, and visibly demonstrated in the lives of your leaders. And you need to memorize the Holy Scriptures that speak to the greatest areas of your weakness or need. As you **Stay The Course**, you will experience **The Abundant Life.** Because it gets better and better! AMEN.

Chapter 6

The Fellowship of Believers

As you follow the leading of the Holy Spirit, the fellowship of believers becomes a blessing, and the new life in Christ grows more abundantly.

It was called, "**The Fellowship.**" This vibrant group of young people all agreeing to assemble and meet on a weekly basis, usually on a Friday or Saturday evening in the home of my Spiritual Mother, not realizing or even caring about the fact that "we were fellowshipping," as we learned the truths of Jesus Christ. This gathering became a mainstay in our interactions and social lives. We grew to love coming together for Bible Study, meaningful discussions, and challenging segments on the application of the Word of God. Sometimes a light meal would follow before the evening closed in prayer.

Initially, the group consisted of all young ladies, who made a vow to become spiritual women of God, rightly dividing the word of truth. No men were allowed. Then, I had the opportunity to lead a young man to Christ and he asked to visit with us. This move eventually led to his brother and other young men who were interested in joining our Bible Study, and we agreed to the change. The age range was from 15 to 22 years old, intelligent, sophisticated, attractive, and quite verbal young men and women.

We were that new generation who would soon grow up to become full-fledged "Baby Boomers," excited about the new opportunities, college education, wealth and success, financial security, material possessions, and everything it takes to have and maintain a rewarding life. Yet, we also craved the desire to have a better understanding of this man who died on the cross for our sins, named Jesus Christ, the Son of God.

These were good times because we began to bond with one another, and challenge each other to grow past our fears and mishaps. We sought to adhere to the deep things of God and began to question church hypocrisy and misconceptions often floating around in the average congregation. Sinful habits and routines became more evident as we examined the Holy Scriptures in contrast to what we experienced at our own church and home environments. We were encouraged to grow beyond our immediate circumstances and learn to trust and depend on the Lord. We cried together, laughed together, and had moments of regret and disappointment together. But, most importantly, we grew up in our relationship with Jesus Christ together, both individually and collectively. The Fellowship produced ministers and friends serving God.

The dialogue was quite stimulating, challenging, and very revealing, which often convicted us of sin, self-righteousness, shame, and outright disobedience. In many instances, I was simply overwhelmed with the depth of my Spiritual Mother's biblical knowledge and lessons of application. She could relate to each one of us on our own level, and then turn around and teach a general lesson that everybody could hear, understand, and accept. We all grew spiritually from her dedication and commitment from **1975 through 1978.** By the early 1980s, many of us were living independently, married, in college, or pursuing our dreams, but we still stayed in contact with her, visiting and sharing stories as we navigated through life.

Let me shout it out loud and clear. Her goal was to "**Make Disciples**" and to teach us to duplicate that process and make more disciples! Jesus initiates the concept of discipleship in the Holy Bible when he says unto them, "Follow me, and I will make you fishers of men," in Matthew 4:19 and Mark 1:17. Discipleship is also mentioned in John 15:16, Colossians 2:6-7, and 2 Timothy 2:2. That was her mandate and she was extremely committed to the cause.

She's in heaven now, as of February 2016. And I know that she is looking down with a smile and saying, "You are all doing just fine; keep on serving God." It's a blessing that I can share with you, that the evidence of her Bible Study ministry is still here, visible, and active on earth.

Many of her students went on to become Sunday school teachers, gospel recording singers, preachers, deacons, missionary workers, pastors, and various leaders in the Christian community—all evangelizing and witnessing for Christ. We got married and had children who are now college graduates. And some of her former students are enjoying the ranks of teaching their grandchildren about the Lord. We are still teaching the Word of God in our families and ministries across the globe. The Lord has His hand on all of us. The fellowship of believers is real, significant, worthwhile, and very productive.

Our fellowship was unique and distinctive. I will never forget it and I will always cherish the special memories. Another thing that I have learned is that the fellowship amongst believers is very important to grow in your relationship with Jesus Christ. It is good to be around other Christians who can share, encourage, and relate to some of the struggles that you're experiencing. You're not merely socializing or just hanging out. You are not alone in the Christian walk.

In fact, the main purpose of going to church is to worship God (John 4:24), to edify/build up one another (Romans 14:19; 1 Corinthians 14:26), and to go back out witnessing in various settings proclaiming the gospel in this wicked world (Acts 1:8). We should be biblically armed and prepared to share the message of Jesus Christ when we work, in our family settings, at social events with friends, and even on our shopping trips (Matthew 28:18-20; Ephesians 6:10-18). As the opportunity is presented, we gain more faith by demonstrating the desire and ability to tell someone else about the goodness of Jesus Christ. The more you do it (witnessing), the easier it becomes. And before long, you will find that striking up a conversation about Jesus Christ gets easier and easier. As the old minister or Baptist preacher hollers, "He walks with me, and talks with me, and tells me that I am His own!" In the days of "The Fellowship," we learned to "practice what was preached," by going out in teams to share the Gospel in our community.

In Hebrews 10:23-25, we are encouraged to hold onto our faith, earnestly love one another promoting good works, and to assemble regularly, which helps to gain strength in these perilous times. Despite the wonderful technological advances that are available for virtual Bible study and church experiences, we still need to come together **face-to-face**. We are commanded to do so in the Name of Jesus Christ. Fellowship was very common amongst the believers in the early church. We learn this in reading the Book of

78

Acts, which provides the exclusive account of the early work of the church. Despite being persecuted and jailed, members of the early church traveled as missionaries to spread the gospel.

After the resurrection of Jesus Christ, the disciples were commanded to go, teach, and baptize in the Name of the Father, Son, and Holy Ghost (Matthew 28:18-20). The directive was given to evangelize throughout the entire world, and bring others into the saving knowledge of Jesus Christ (Acts 1:8). We are supposed to teach people to teach and duplicate that process, thereby spreading the Gospel of Jesus Christ.

Another benefit from the fellowship of believers is that it helps us to focus on repentance and rebuke sin. As we turn away from toxic relationships (people who don't mean us any good) and release bad habits and negativity, we are able to build a bond of emotional support and safety. Sin begins to "drop off," as we continue to lead people to Jesus Christ and become doers of the will of God. Our labor in building up the kingdom of God becomes more meaningful as described in Acts 2:37-40. Eventually, the common bond that develops will bring us to function on **One Accord**. We become like-minded in thought and deed.

We begin to eat together, pray together, share, and distribute our wealth and possessions to one another. The growth pattern is obvious as God receives praise and glory. He is magnified and begins to add to the church those who will be saved, as it is mentioned in Acts 2:41-47. The Bible clearly states that there was fellowship from house to house with gladness and singleness of heart. In today's modern church settings, you will find a whole gamut of "special days" that include: church/pastor anniversaries, birthday celebrations, community outreach, bowling groups, skating parties, youth events, community awareness, and health fairs, senior support programs, prayer breakfasts, musicals, and concerts, programs for persons with special needs or disabilities, clothing drives, and so much more. What a wonderful thing it is when the people of God truly come together for the right reason, the right purpose, and of course, at the right time!

As fellowship continues (in your personal relationship and with other believers), you will be hated. You will experience persecutions, troubles, afflictions, sufferings, and tribulations, all for the sake of Jesus Christ. Because you identify with Him, the world will not like you, as mentioned in Matthew 5:11, Luke 6:22, and John 15:18-19. This is a known fact, **once you begin** the Christian journey. Of course, I was not told this part, at the beginning of my **serious walk** with God. Probably because I was already having enough problems! I was already in the heat of my personal battles! I was struggling and trying to figure things out.

Yet, in spite of the suffering, the power of God resides in the heart of the believer, enabling them to overcome every situation and be delivered as mentioned in 2 Corinthians 4:7-10, 2 Corinthians 12:9-10, and in 2 Timothy 3:10-12. As the Apostle Paul stated, "His grace is sufficient."

The early church believers, members, participants, or congregants, learned to overcome every mountain and obstacle by showing true love. We find that many miracles, signs, and wonders bring the fulfillment of joy. And peace of mind resulted from genuine forgiveness and sweet expressions of the love of God.

Love conquers a multitude of sins, differences, and misunderstandings as described in 1 Peter 4:8-9 and 1 Corinthians 13. The compassion of Jesus Christ is vividly recorded throughout the Gospels (Matthew, Mark, Luke, and John). And, as believers and fellow members of the Body of Christ, we should exhibit oneness and Christ-like features, attitudes, behaviors, and the mindset to love one another as described in Ephesians 4:22-23 and in Philippians 2:1-4, 12-15.

I really want to emphasize this point because we are all members of the Body of Christ. That's right! Every Christian is a member of the Body of Christ, with a specific role, gift(s), or part to play. There are many gifts, talents, and skills to serve God, according to the measure of grace given to each person, exclusively by the Holy Spirit. This is stated in detail when you read 1 Corinthians 12:4-11. Believe it or not, you have a spiritual gift if you are a child of God. Therefore, every Christian has a definite ministry, which is discussed in-depth in 1 Corinthians 12:12-31. The fulfillment of a good ministry is exercised in love as explained in the Love chapter, 1 Corinthians 13. As you begin to cultivate your spiritual gift, God will open up opportunities for you to serve Him. It is a personal statement of growth, faith, development, and a desire to bring others into the saving knowledge and admonition of Jesus Christ.

The Fellowship finally came to a halt as we began to explore other areas to become well-rounded citizens and adults. Some of us got married, went off to a seminary, became more active in church, moved to other states for employment, and relocated to attend college or graduate school. Although we all went our separate ways, we remained connected to that special woman who had influenced our lives. We continued to give her individual updates on our progress. We valued her insight on life circumstances and respected her tutelage.

For me, as I've said, I married my high school sweetheart and we started our new life together in 1978 as a married couple.

Everything was peaches, cream, honey, ice cream, and cake. I loved being a wife and a new mother while navigating around New York, a huge city that never went to sleep. We lived on Staten Island and commuted by ferry every day to Manhattan, for school, work, and social activities. It was an amazing time in our lives. Neither of us had any extended family members or friends in our new setting. We were alone, but together chasing our dreams for success. However, we left out the most important piece to the marriage puzzle. The component that is necessary. The missing ingredient that can settle differences and weather any storm. God. God has the answer to every problem.

We did not adhere to our church covenant (from our original source back home) and connect with another church in our new location. God was on the back burner of our lives. He became second place. And many years later after my divorce, after raising our daughter, and dealing with life as a single woman, my Spiritual Mother and I had a long discussion about "what really happened to our marriage." It was a rude awakening. It was enlightening and cleansing, while serving as a great catharsis. To this day, whenever the opportunity presents itself, I tell every couple, whether they're young or old, to "**keep God in your marriage**." That is the real difference between failure and success. He makes the difference between understanding or disruption. But **life goes on** and we grow from strength to strength as shown in Psalms 84:7-12. The moral of the story is to keep on living the Christian life.

As I shared with you before, time, distance, and chance happen to all, as it is distinctly recorded in Ecclesiastes 9:11. The motivation to keep our marriage together became insurmountable and led to divorce. It was a big letdown.

It took time for me to personally grow at this stage of my Christian life because I was used to being by myself before The Fellowship, and by now, after the marital breakup, I felt so alone. As a young child, I grew up in a household with four brothers, so I always stood out as "a girl." I stayed focused to please my parents, adhering to their don'ts about growing up, finishing college, not getting pregnant before marriage, treating others right, and staying away from drugs. I listened intently to their warnings to "don't do this and don't do that."

I believe that my mother psychologically trained me by saying, "Regina, be intelligent!" I guess that's why my favorite word is "Excellent." It was instilled into my senses at a very early age to be a high achiever, reach your goals, do well, and live a good, wholesome life. Coupled with the fact that my years of Bible study had revealed God's Way for truth, hope, faith, and reality, despite a dismal world.

It was a bummer to be a divorcée and a single mom. The happily ever after marriage ended and exposed my weaknesses. I had no desire to fellowship with other Christians. There was no visible road map that laid out the ABC's on how to live a successful, single life as a Christian woman. I was unhappy about being a divorcée and having the responsibility to raise our daughter. All my dreams of togetherness were shattered! We had grown up together since age 16 and I didn't know which way to turn. I did not have a "Plan B." Marriage was supposed to work! I was very disappointed, hurt, rejected, angry, and now alone at the prime of my life. I was 29 years old, still trying to figure things out.

It was a difficult and sad time for me because I was used to the joy, fun, freedom, excitement, security, and pleasure of the marital bond. I tried to hide my sin and still function in the church, but it made me feel guilty and shy, causing me to stay away from regular "Christian circles of communication and fellowship." Many members in my local church were blood-related (cousins, uncles, sisters and brothers, and so on). They always seemed to know everything going on within the church walls. I felt like an outsider most of the time. I could sing well, I loved God, and I was growing in the Lord. While I had a few friends, I stayed in my own little world. My peers and colleagues were not complaining and seemed to be doing fine in their marriages and pursuits.

It "appeared," like everyone else was doing well, too. But the reality became more and more apparent in my surroundings as I noticed discrepancies, open disagreements, some character flaws, outbursts, and church conflict.

However, time has a way of healing all wounds, and I slowly started to fellowship with more confidence and the certainty that God would take care of me. I gradually participated in some of the church programs and events. I learned to say, "Lord, I trust you," quietly to myself whenever I was afraid. He will never leave nor forsake you, as stated in Hebrews 13:5-6. The Lord is my helper and guide.

In all of our churches, you will find regular people who are sinners saved by His Grace as stated in Ephesians 2:8-9. Some may be hypocrites, backbiters, mean-spirited liars, cheaters, and so on. They come from a variety of backgrounds, habits, and values. Some people have been well disciplined, while others may have a long list of dysfunctional behavior. The world's influence on social interaction may be a negative force that causes well-intended souls to go astray.

You may witness a host of "cliques," which can be troublesome, but the grace of God will sustain and keep you steady in church.

Remember, the church of God will prevail. The blood of our Lord and Savior, Jesus Christ, covers us and He presents us faultless before the throne of God. The Holy Spirit is our Comforter, teacher, and guide. That is why we need to depend solely upon our high priest, the Son of God, who was touched with the same hurts and infirmities that we experience, and who can directly relate to each of our needs. We can come boldly before the throne of grace to obtain mercy and help as discussed in Hebrews 4:14-16. The opportunity to build solid, wholesome relationships with believers is important. You can open your arms and receive, as well as give love. You can be delivered from the bondage of sin and have the confidence of joy, peace, harmony, and good fortune.

I am convinced that the fellowship of believers is summed up in one beautiful phrase, "One Accord." It simply means like-mindedness, to be unified with genuine concern, to maintain kindred spirits, while caring and sharing with kindness to one another. I encourage you to accept the challenge, grow stronger in your relationship with Jesus Christ, and the bond from Christian fellowship. Stay active in a Bible-believing/teaching church ministry and watch the process lead you to a greater understanding of **The Abundant Christian Life.**

Living for Jesus

Chapter 7

New Life, More Abundantly

THIS IS A GREAT chapter because I get to tell you about all of the wonderful things that God has done in my life. I am grateful for the abundant life, where love, joy, peace, longsuffering, gentleness, goodness, meekness, faith, and self-control guide my daily walk with God.

There are so many scriptures about life in the Holy Bible. This new life in Jesus Christ is described as the ultimate goal for Christians. It's a special gift because not only does it offer eternal life after physical death, but it provides an abundant life as we live, right here, and right now on earth! It's almost an oxymoron, where you get to experience blessings and the peace of God, as you walk closely with Him. Then when you die, you go to heaven and live with God the Father, forever. Depending on where you are when you say, "Yes to Jesus," has a significant impact on your level of growth, development, and commitment. Whether or not you come to Christ emotionally banged up, self-righteous but seeking, or functioning pretty well, the abundant Christian life is a life of **sacrifice, sanctification, separation, steadfastness, and service.**

I used to think that people who were rich and famous had the best kind of life. We live in a society that constantly projects images of wealth, success, fame, and fortune through the media, entertainment, sports, and digital technology. We're bombarded constantly with the latest new gadget from marketing experts, who prey on consumer tastes and needs every day. Their strategy in promoting new trends in society is overwhelming. When I was growing up, the popular phrase was "Keeping up with the Joneses." Just because your neighbor had it, you wanted it, too! That game of comparing and contrasting has played on the emotions and pocketbooks of many people searching for an abundant life. The vicious cycle of obtaining more and more material things creates frustration, as we chase the elusive ghost hoping for the abundant life. Then finally it hits us, smack-dab in the face, that life is still miserable, even with all the possessions that we have accumulated over time. The money, popularity, fame, cars, vacations, boats, houses, and stuff no longer satisfy that deep longing to be whole and free. We find out that it's not true, but a real joke, and that it's frivolous. A huge disappointment.

For many people, it's like shock therapy. The world is not what it initially appeared to be. It really sucks. And we often proclaim, "I am sick and tired of this syndrome. Is there anything better?" Well, let me introduce you to Jesus Christ! It was like a jolt that hit me and saved me from my own personal destruction. The road to success, joy, peace, and harmony is found in a yielded life to the Way, Will, Wisdom, and Word of God. Are you tired of wasting time, running around in circles of spiritual defeat? Let's get started so that you can have an abundant life, too!

Jesus says in John 10:10, "The thief cometh not, but for to steal, kill and destroy; I am come that they might have life, and that they might have it more abundantly." In the next verse (10:11), He says that he is the good shepherd who gives His life for the sheep. In John

3:15-17, Jesus says that whosoever believes in Him will have eternal life and not perish. He claims that he was sent to save the world, not to condemn the world. The Apostle Paul states boldy in 2 Corinthians 5:7, "Therefore, if any man be in Christ, he is a new creature; old things are passed away; behold, all things are become new."

In Luke 12:15, Jesus states that a man's life does not consist in the abundance of the things he possesses. And in Matthew 6:33, He admonishes us to first seek the kingdom of God and His righteousness, and everything else we need will be added to our lives. Your life belongs to God.

As you begin to live for Jesus, you begin to make the **sacrifices** necessary to demonstrate a yielded Christian life. This is primarily displayed in your attitude and behavior to reject sin and its dominion over you. You will sacrifice and learn to say, "No thank you, Satan." It is presented as no longer serving sin as stated in Romans 6:6-10. You will no longer obey the sensual lusts of the flesh, attempting to lure you back into the clutches of evil as described in Romans 6:11-13. As a young, newly single mother, I memorized Galatians 2:20-21 to guard my heart against the traps of the enemy. It says, "I am crucified with Christ; nevertheless I live; yet not I, but Christ lives in me; and the life which I now live in the flesh live by the faith of the Son of God, who loved me and gave himself for me." I can vividly remember the good times during childhood because my dear parents sacrificed to make sure that our home was warm, comfortable, and full of love.

You may have had that experience as well. Yet, nothing compares to the sacrifice of Jesus Christ. The abundant life appreciates everything that He did on Calvary's Cross to reconcile our relationship with Almighty God.

You will sacrifice your life to represent Jesus Christ as stated in Romans 12:1-2, by presenting your body as a living sacrifice, holy and acceptable unto God being transformed by the powerful Word of God. Words of praise become a regular focus as you speak about the goodness of God as stated in Hebrews 13:15-16. I found myself saying, "Thank you, Jesus, Praise the Lord, Hallelujah, We bless Your Name," on a regular basis. The joy of the Lord became more evident in my life as I grew closer to the Lord. My prayers were answered. I began to experience this inner peace, feeling whole again. I want to pause here, because rejection, disappointment, hurt, crazy people, envy, jealousy, bitterness, heartache, and defeat can take a toll on all of us.

Relax and trust only God. He is the deliverer and will fight your battles, one by one, like He did in 2 Chronicles 20:15-17. So, we must thank God for the sacrifice of Jesus Christ, who was wounded for our transgressions and His blood paid the penalty for our sin (Isaiah 53:4-6). Thank you, Jesus, for keeping my life safe from all physical hurt, intentional harm, and sudden danger. You are my rock and my shield (2 Samuel 22:2-3). Don't you want to have an abundant life full of joy, peace, and love?

The abundant life is where you **begin to live for Jesus.** Living for Jesus is an exciting time as you walk with the Lord sacrificing your time, talent, and treasure. Yes, we are encouraged to give generously to others, do good, and seek those opportunities to share our wealth with the people of God as mentioned in Romans 12:8-16 and Hebrews 13:16. We are encouraged to overcome evil with good, at all costs, as we demonstrate the love of God (Romans 12:17-21). Instead of walking around in shame, you can take off your mask, trust God, and walk in victory. We are encouraged to love one another, help each other, to be generous, hospitable, kind, and living in harmony as Christians and as believers willing to obey God. Your personal goals focus to line up with God's will for your life.

That is the example "the world" needs to see. And it starts with You. I decided to examine my own facts, faults, frailties, and failures. I desperately wanted to have this abundant life promised in His Word (Psalms 112).

So, I began to search and present myself as a willing, yielded, and teachable vessel to learn His methods and procedures for living this great life. Ironically, it's all right there in the Bible, but it seems like it takes forever to get to that realization.

There are so many distractions that can impede your progress. As I applied myself, my overall **stewardship** got better and I got better. This led to a deeper understanding of **sanctification and separation**. I began to accept that being sanctified is not consumed in a set pattern of rules and regulations condemning your outward appearance. My mother used to say that she and her favorite cousin used to go and sing at "sanctified churches," in the South, where you couldn't do this, or wear that, and how strict the religious services were during her childhood. You see, mankind looks on the outside, but God looks inside your heart.

A person's holiness is not guaranteed by covering your head, or **not wearing** lipstick or tight clothing, shorts, mini-skirts, backless dresses, too-tight jeans, low-cut blouses or shirts, and nail polish. He shows each one of us our own sinful ways that relate to showing oneself indiscreetly, provoking a healthy change. Remember, God looks at your heart as mentioned in 1 Samuel 16:7. However, you never want to be a stumbling block and prevent another Christian from growing closer to God (1 Corinthians 6:12, 8:9). We travel this journey expediently, not to offend others. Your goal, eventually, is **to please** God!

The term sanctified or **sanctification** means, "to be set apart." As you study the course of abundant living, there is a desire to honor God with your words, character, thoughts, attitude, and actions. Your outward behavior will become an attractive feature displaying your true, inward character. The need to "dress to impress" the world will leave your mindset and you will dress to impress the Kingdom of God. Given that my body belongs to Jesus, I decided to carry myself in a wholesome manner, looking as beautiful as possible, often. It was not for a man, not for mankind, and not even to boast, but to display the beautiful person that God made in creating me. He describes this in Psalms 139, one of my favorite passages in the Bible. My speech became clearer and more distinct. I began to tell others about Jesus with confidence and conviction. Through witnessing to others, and sharing the love of God at church events, it became evident to some and a surprise to others that greater things were in store for me. I was on my way to serving God with peace, joy, enthusiasm, and while having my life intact.

To be **sanctified** means to consecrate yourself to be used by God for His purpose as He does amazing work in your life. He will pull you away from sinful habits and towards Christian virtues. Jesus asked the Father to sanctify his followers by the truth in His great intercessory prayer found in John 17:17-19. The truth will always make you free (John 8:32). The Apostle Paul so eloquently writes that we are sanctified in Christ Jesus, called to be saints the moment we accept Him as our Lord and Savior (1 Corinthians 1:2-9). This is our standing in Jesus Christ as we grow in grace through our walk with Him.

We are to grow up in the Lord fulfilling our part in the body of Christ, edifying one another in the spirit of love (Ephesians 4:14-16). The abundant life comes from adhering to this principle and exercising the discipline necessary to demonstrate its power. The **separation** from the world is mandatory. That's a fact.

Now, I don't mean mandatory in a derogatory way. But mandatory in a healthy style where you **crave to do the right thing,** the best thing, the most beneficial thing, as often as possible. First of all, we are called to be separate and to live a holy life as given in Romans 1:1 and 1 Peter 1:15-16. Where there is darkness, you become the light. Where there is pain, your presence brings in the joy. Where you see disappointment, you encourage others to trust in the Lord. The desire is to live righteously, given that God has reconciled us to himself by Jesus Christ as stated in 2 Corinthians 5:18-21. The abundant life summons you to come out from associating with "the world," and be separate for the glory of God, our heavenly Father (2 Corinthians 6:17-18). Your personal habits definitely change.

The Sermon on the Mount is given by Jesus Christ in three chapters: Matthew 5, 6, and 7. Here, the Lord tells his disciples (the 12 and a multitude of listeners) to love enemies. He teaches them to pray, and that they are the salt of the earth and the light of the world. He instructs them to bless those who curse them, to give to others, and do so much more. The abundant life becomes all-encompassing as you adapt to the ways of God and move further from the ways of the world (Matthew 5-7). We have to be careful, wise, and faithful because **sin can separate us from God,** which causes Him to turn away from hearing us, as described in Isaiah 59:2. That is why we must confess our sins every day to regain and maintain communication and fellowship with God.

My Spiritual Mother encouraged me to memorize 1 John 1:9. It says, "If we confess our sins, he is faithful and just to forgive us our sins, and to cleanse us from all unrighteousness." And to be candid with you, (honestly speaking) I didn't really start **practicing this doctrine consistently** until January 25, 2015. That is a significant date in my Christian life because it is the day that my new Pastor and spiritual leader preached his first sermon at the church where I served faithfully.

It was at my local church in the neighborhood not too far from my family's residence. It was the place where "church" became a real entity in our lives. My parents were members, while my brothers (except one), and I had been there since **1968**. My youngest brother, who was handicapped, attended another church that was wheelchair accessible and located down the street from where we lived. Upon the new preacher's arrival, I told my Spiritual Mother, "I'll know within 30 days if he is going to be my new Pastor." I was at a personal standstill in my spiritual walk with God and needed to be challenged to grow in faith. The health of my Spiritual Mother was failing and conversations with her were more intense, significant, meaningful, and reminiscent about our spiritual bond over the years. She knew that God was calling her name and preparing her to go to the heavenly home. And she also knew that her student (favorite... smile), needed to be stimulated, pushed, reminded, and challenged to grow to the next level in walking with God.

The inner workings of our congregation had slowly deteriorated over a four-year period as our elderly Senior Pastor grew ill. There were problems that included internal division, mockery, mixed messages, discrepancies, unbelief circulating, verbal disputes, and the entire church environment was distracted like the church described in 1 Corinthians 3:3. And, even though I love to sing, the choir was growing stale and sour, singing the same old songs! Sunday morning services depicted the stench of a group of people who were "just going through the motions."

I was not getting the spiritual food that I needed to experience the fullness of joy described in Psalms 16:11 and John 16:22-24. From my position, things seemed to boil down to one special program after the other, for some special group in the church to socialize. Sadly, the atmosphere was dull, boring, and mundane. The attendance was very low. I was definitely ready for a new, refreshing change in the total atmosphere. I yearned for a new direction that would impact the future growth of the church.

It was a well-known, established church within the city of Detroit. Our Pastor was known as a faithful Preacher and teacher throughout the nation. He was influential in political, civic, and religious circles. In addition, we had a viable music department on each level with strong leadership and experience, and a variety of Christian Ministries operating in the church. The longevity for most of the congregants was a plus, averaging 15, 20, 30, or more years.

We used official election booths to select our new Pastor, who was very enthusiastic, energetic, and Biblically sound. He also preached feverishly. He expounded on the Word of God with knowledge and depth, and he shared openly. During his sermons, he stayed with the subject matter and did not go off on a tangent. He also challenged each member in the congregation to check their spiritual thermometer, and determine where they were going in their walk with God.

I immediately began to listen, observe, respond, and review the scriptures that were used in every sermon. He talked about repentance, and turning away from sin, forgiveness, and making it a point to confess your sins daily as you walk with God. Under his teachings in Bible Study and preaching on Sunday mornings, a new effervescent, refreshing attitude began to grow in my spirit. I became invigorated, revived, and restored to attempt to move beyond my fears and leap with faith to trust this new process. It was time for a new change, and to embrace it with God's blessing.

After my own personal 30-day evaluation of his preaching style, approach, consistency, and directness, I was convinced that God had led him and his wife to **my** city to help **me** grow in **my relationship with God**. My observations were confirmed by his depth, strength, and expanded knowledge of the holy scriptures.

He delivered a thorough and complete presentation of the Gospel of Jesus Christ. I told my Spiritual Mother and my daughter that I was completely satisfied and "can see myself," moving forward. The abundant life was mine! I chose to believe in nothing more, nothing less, and nothing else; except a new approach to ministry under a new leader who came with new ideas and new methods. The fire lit deep inside my soul and I was bubbling over with new ideas for the ministry.

Unfortunately, however, newness isn't always nice, especially when a group of people have functioned in a church with the same, old habits and traditions for more than 50 years. Change, although forthcoming, was hard and difficult for some members to accept. That discomfort with the new and familiarity with the past led to the disruptive, unlawful dismissal of our new leader. I found myself torn, but motivated to take on the uncertainty of moving forward, despite the conflict!

After three years of serving as our new pastor and leader (2015-2018), the church's by-laws were changed, to ensure that the disgruntled members could get rid of him. What they did was not in accordance with the original by-laws of the church and it was unjust. It was a nasty affair with legal ramifications. It was very disgraceful and exposed some personality traits of individuals that were hidden. I was very frustrated and angry because I had started growing spiritually and consistently under our new Pastor. Also, there were many other members, who were angry with that decision. It was unfair, unjust, ungodly, and unwarranted. It was mean! I have seen and personally experienced meanness in my life, as I shared with you in earlier chapters. Yet, the power of God always overrides any man-made decision. That's why I can say, "But for the grace of God. He is the deliverer," as mentioned in Jeremiah 1:8. God was **with** my new Pastor **and** on his side! You're not going to believe what happened next in this true story.

God had a better plan waiting in close proximity, and immediately delivered us into a place to worship and serve Him. Then within a matter of a few weeks, His sovereign power ushered in a completely furnished church for us to continue serving, praising, worshipping, and giving to the Kingdom of God under this great new Pastor whom I had grown to respect and love. It was a miracle, like a dream come true. Almost unbelievable, but it was happening right in front of my eyes!

I am so thankful that God still hears and answers the prayers of the righteous. The eyes of the Lord are upon the righteous, and his ears are open unto their cry, according to Psalms 34:15-17. God heard our cries and prayers and yearnings. He delivered my Pastor and faithful congregants, and led us to victory. As a result, my service to the Lord continued with gratitude, thanksgiving, and faithfulness to God under the man of God who watches for my soul, as given in Hebrews 13:17. Our heavenly Father always leads, heals, guides, protects, and strengthens His believers.

You'll know that abundant life has become your reality when the fighting starts. The war going on inside will tell you to swing back with all of your strength, to scream and holler, to push and pull the best punch. But the voice of the Holy Spirit will whisper in your ear, "Therefore my beloved brethren, be steadfast, unmovable, always abounding in the work of the Lord," as stated in 1 Corinthians 15:58. Or He might say, "Let your light so shine before men that they will see your good works and glorify the father which is heaven," which is presented in Matthew 5:16. Or some other scripture will come to your mind and tell you not to be anxious, but to hold on and keep the peace of God as stated in Philippians 4:6-7.

Keep on praying and believing in Him. God is not dead. He is still on the throne and in control of everything, as proclaimed in Psalms 24, written by King David. God is the King of Glory! The Lord strong and mighty, the Lord mighty in battle. As your strength increases, you will remain steadfast.

The abundant life includes being **steadfast.** To be steadfast is to be firm in purpose, faith, and loyalty. According to Webster's Pocket Dictionary, it means to be unwavering, constant, and dependable. This includes being firmly fixed in faith or devotion to duty. We learn in 1 Peter 5:8-9, that we can resist the wiles of the devil (Satan) as we remain steadfast in the faith. We're not ignorant of his tactics, trickery, or devices as stated in 2 Corinthians 2:11: as he walks this earth looking for those who can be eaten up or defeated.

Neither are we subject to fear because God has not given us the spirit of fear, but of power, love, and of a sound mind as recorded in 1 Timothy 1:7.

Therefore, we can participate in the afflictions and persecutions of the gospel of Jesus Christ as we walk with God, holding onto His promises. In James 4:7 we are told to submit to God, then we **can resist** the devil and **he will flee (RUN)** from us. Now that's truly a bold statement to grasp.

As you experience the abundant life, you will become unmovable, always abounding in the work of the Lord, knowing that your labor—Christian work, service, or ministry—is not in vain, as mentioned in 2 Corinthians 15:58. As you remain steadfast, the peaks and valleys become less of a nuisance and more of a welcome. You will realize that this is a life-long journey. No one on Earth knows everything. And no one person can demonstrate absolute perfection in the Christian life. However, the maturity that becomes obvious to you, will become noticeable to others who are watching your every step. I believe when a person matures spiritually, they mature in their overall demeanor as a human being. My parents and my Spiritual Mother also agreed with that fact.

Your purpose is defined and your endeavors become worthwhile, which benefits others who cross your path. It is a wonderful feeling knowing that you have something to contribute for improving and edifying the Body of Christ (Believers, Christians, Brothers and Sisters in Christ). This trend will lead you to make a very important decision. At some point, at some stage, the Holy Spirit will help you to declare, pronounce, and seek to develop your spiritual gift(s). And that, my friend, is a featured highlight of the abundant life. The performance will begin as your desire to serve the Lord gladly takes off. And here is **"Where the fun begins!"** Love, learn, listen, and live as the Spirit dictates your next move.

Let me tell you about the service of the Lord as you experience the abundant life. The abundant life draws you to a life of **Christian service**. A pull on you that cannot be ignored or repressed will constantly come up. It is the voice of the Holy Spirit saying, "You need to be serving God in a greater capacity." You'll begin to think about how to do it. Questions will arise, such as, "Where can I serve and in what capacity? Who's going to help train me? God, are you really sure that you're speaking to me? When am I going to get the chance? What shall I do? Where can I obtain the tools that I need for ministry?" Wait, trust, believe, and stay ready. Before you look, the process will unfold elevating you.

The abundant life leads you to discover and exercise your spiritual gift(s) to serve the Lord. We all have a unique gift given by the power of the Holy Spirit. Some believers have more than one gift, based solely upon God's will for their particular place and platform in ministry. This is the stage in your Christian walk where you serve God in a greater capacity, fully committed to the promotion of the gospel of Jesus Christ. Your joy will become full. In the Holy Bible, there's a complete list of the spiritual gifts, specifically in Romans 12 and 1 Corinthians 12-14. In these chapters, you will find the outline of the gifts of the Holy Spirit, their function, and purpose in the Body of Christ. As you pray, study, and listen to the voice of God, you'll be led into your direct purpose for service.

After studying with my Spiritual Mother for approximately three years, I knew that I had the gift of exhortation and teaching. I began to exercise both gifts in small Bible studies with those whom I had led to Jesus Christ. I was also encouraging others to trust and believe God to work out their concerns and circumstances. I was anticipating more Christian responsibility, so I took a few courses at a local Bible college. Singing in the church choir was great at that time, but I knew God was calling me to do more. Yet my commitment to service in ministry, mission, or purpose for God was put on hold due to getting married and starting a family, moving to New York City, and launching my career goals.

I've already shared with you the anguish I felt after my marriage ended. However, I think that the divorce was the first time in my life that I ever felt the deep, throbbing pain of hurt and rejection that wouldn't go away. My anger towards God, my ex-spouse, other couples doing well, and even my Spiritual Mother, depleted the energy to seek God. I was sad, bitter, unsure, humiliated, disappointed, and miserable. I felt like I had lost my way.

However, our heavenly Father always has a "ram in the bush," (see Genesis 22:12-13 and 1 Corinthians 10:13) to deliver us out of every hurtful situation. I moved back home to live with my parents and to raise our daughter. One day after observing my sad, strange countenance, my father said, "Why don't you go back to church and sing in the choir?" He knew that I needed to do something "else" that I really loved, instead of moping and sitting around the house.

And that is exactly what I did. That one step was the springboard that launched my desire to get back on the right track, evaluate where I was going next, and recommit to trusting God. You cannot, I repeat cannot, live the abundant Christian life in your own strength. It really doesn't matter how smart you are or how much money you make. It is totally impossible. Nothing compares to the grace and knowledge of Jesus Christ. Nothing compares to the majestic power of God to forgive us, clean us up, and get us going into a new, positive direction. It is best described in Psalms 51:10-13, where King David cries out, "Create in me a clean heart, O God, and renew a right spirit within me."

In fact, the year was **1987**, when I went back to my home church, still located in the neighborhood. They were planning and preparing for a major concert featuring the Minister of Music, local musicians, and the combined choirs of the church at a citywide venue. It was an exciting performance, and I sang a special solo leading the choir with, "I've Come A Long Way But I Still Have a Long Way to Go!" That particular song spoke to my heart, my situation, and my desire to keep moving forward despite the faltering in my personal Christian journey. It helped me gain a new perspective. As my desire grew to turn things over to the Lord, the more I faced sin knocking at my door, trying to keep me in bondage. I began to draw from the wealth of scriptures that I had memorized a long time ago in Bible Study. They were hidden deep in my heart and I needed to start the process of healing—emotionally, mentally, financially, and spiritually.

At this point, I began to realize that my life belonged to God and he was my sustainer. I learned that his grace is sufficient for all of life's circumstances and that "I can do all things through Christ who strengthens me" (Philippians 4:13). I can resist temptation, refrain from following evil, and monitor my conversations. By submitting to God, I could resist the devil (1 Peter 5:8), and keep iniquity from creeping easily back into my life. I did not want my prayers hindered (Psalms 66:18). **Service** to the Lord means to use every opportunity that presents itself as a chance to show forth Jesus Christ and His goodwill in your life. Your problems are not handled in an immature fashion, but are managed by the awesome power of God. By praying diligently, regularly, and sincerely, you will become an example of someone who represents a holy, righteous lifestyle (James 5:16). As you seek God for repentance and instructions in ministry, you may find it necessary to fast and pray as they did in Acts 14:21-25. The work of the Lord often requires the extraordinary in your efforts to reach people and spread the love of God.

As you grow to trust God, He will open up the windows, the doors, and gates to allow you to exercise your spiritual gift(s) in **Christian service.** You may be asked to volunteer to pray in a meeting, or lead a song, or assist in some other tasks. Then considerable requests will come as God uses you more and more. When this happens, you will be so grateful and fully aware of the wisdom that results from trusting in Him. You will shout "Hallelujah," because you have been chosen by God to represent His great Message of Salvation, The Abundant Life, and Eternal Life to the lost souls in this world.

In my relationship with God, I have the mindset now where I can boldly exclaim, just like the Apostle Paul did in Philippians 1:21 many years ago, "For me to live is Christ, and to die is gain." This book is the outgrowth of my own spiritual walk with God. And I pray that you have made the decision **to get started, to grow, and to reach** for the stars as you **stay with it,** and **serve the Lord** with gladness.

When you do, **Your Mission, Ministry, and Purpose to Serve** in the Christian life is waiting for you to assume and take control. Then you will experience the joy and fulfillment of **Living for Jesus Christ!**

Chapter 8

Mission, Ministry, To Serve with Purpose

In Matthew 6:33, Jesus Christ says, "But, seek ye first the kingdom of God, and his righteousness, and all these things shall be added unto you." It is a command that tells us to search for ways to expand, promote, and cultivate a climate that manifests the Word of God in the hearts of every man, woman, boy and girl. This is the main thing that we should do as a believer, as a Christian, as a child of God. It is the first priority and nothing should take precedence over that directive. The part that says, "and all these things" refers to the many things in life that we wish for, need, want, and desire. So many things have very little to do with Salvation, but we crave as we're seeking the cares of this world. Food, shelter, clothing, vacations, education, riches, houses, land, sex, money, fame, and fortune often capture our attention.

In the earlier verses, Jesus describes how the lilies and birds are cared for by God (Matthew 6:25-29). We as human beings are also cared for by God. He encourages us to not worry about anything because God knows our needs and will take care of us (Matthew

6:30-34). This is the grace of God as manifested through faith in Jesus Christ and living within us by the power of the Holy Spirit (Ephesians 2:8-9; John 14:15-18).

To begin to serve God is the **Mission.** You begin to serve Him with your mind, heart, soul, and body (Mark 12:28-30). Whatever the task, whenever the opportunity arises, and however it occurs, you aim to glorify God when asked to serve. It is an honor and privilege to lend your skills, talents, and gifts to God. He will never disappoint you and will never leave you hopeless (Hebrews 13:5-6). He will hold your hand every step of the way. You learn to walk by faith, and experience a deeper sense of God's presence in your life, actions, responsibilities, and deeds (2 Corinthians 5:7). You begin to "hear His voice," and you really start to listen and apply the Word of God regularly, not just every now and then or occasionally. The abundant life, which is "the better life," becomes your reality right here on earth. You'll find yourself acting peculiar, different, open-minded, kind, humble, more understanding of others, and able to function freely just like it's stated in Titus 2:11-14 and 1 Peter 2:9.

As my Pastor says, "He is your God, your guide, your guard and your gauge as you travel the Christian journey. He will lead, protect, strengthen, and comfort you."

Your mission, task, or duty will become clearer, the moment you declare, discover, develop, and initiate your spiritual gift(s). This is the indicator of your desire and willingness to be used by God in ministry. Your mission will directly coincide with the Great Commission that was given by Jesus Christ himself, in Matthew 28:18-20. We must surrender to the will of God, accept His plan and move according to His purpose for your life. This is the cost of discipleship as described in Luke 9:23-26 and Ephesians 5:1-2. The first and most important thing we are supposed to do is to "**Go.**" Then Jesus said we should "**teach.**" And finally, "**baptize them,**" in the Name of the Father, and of the Son, and of the Holy Spirit. We should teach them—people, sinners, the lost, the backslidden, the carnal folk, etc.—to observe all of the words that Jesus spoke. And He promises to be with us always, even until the end of the world. Notice, He does not say, "just go to church." You won't find that statement in the Bible, at all. Yes, we gain a lot from our local church fellowship, however the role of the church is not just to sit and be taught. The charge is to go and make disciples! **That** is our primary role.

Before I talk about ministry and the various ways you can operate in your spiritual gifts, I'd like to discuss hindrances which can impede the discovery process. Although you may experience a pull or nudge encouraging you to serve God, (which is, by the way the Holy Spirit), you may be **too busy.** When we get involved in too many things, this can prevent you from following the guidance of the Holy Spirit. For example, your work assignments, special events, important meetings, socializing, and even family demands can get in the way. They become obstacles. Therefore, it is important to set aside time to pray. You have to be specific, intentional, and go out of your way to meet God at the altar with a sincere heart and open mind. Second of all, the **bondage of sin** can disrupt your desire to develop your spiritual gift and serve in ministry. There is sin of commission, what you know you have done, and sin of omission, the things you should have done but refused to do, and sin of things that you're unaware of, yet still committed.

That's why we need to adhere to the scripture in 1 John 1:9, which admonishes us to confess our sin daily. Then, we must repent and turn away from sin, by exercising discipline and incorporating new, healthy habits into our lifestyle. Then, you must beware of **pride** and **vainglory**. Don't get caught off guard when you begin to receive praise, success, accolades, applause, and compliments about how well you functioned in a church service capacity. My dear, Spiritual Mother specifically reminded me to always say, "Praise the Lord," whenever I would receive compliments from singing. She said, "Always give the glory and honor to God because it will keep you from getting puffed up with pride."

Pride can kill any good intention and leave a person doubting their ability and confidence and it leads to a fall. Boasting, bragging, and being arrogant can induce pretentious behavior. We are clearly warned about this trait through many Biblical examples, and especially in the book of Proverbs 6:16-19, 16:18, 27:1-3, and 29:23. God hates pride. It's one of seven abominations unto Him. It is a destructive element to be aware of as you pursue ministry.

If you are a **poor listener**, then I believe that your growth in the area of developing your mission, ministry, and service to God can be delayed. When seeking confirmation and suggestions from other spiritually-minded leaders, it is so important to listen to their words. They can give you insight into your approach, style, demeanor, or delivery which can foster continued growth and development. Listen with the "third ear" to what they did not say and relate it to what you have heard "God say" to you. The quiet time is necessary to hear the voice of the Holy Spirit, as he guides your every step and move. When I am still, I hear God better. His word says, "be still and know that I am God; I will be exalted among the nations, I will be exalted in the earth," in Psalms 46:10.

Finally, you must **seek His face** as you're discovering your spiritual gift. Seek his guidance and position for your life. Seek his leading and direction to that specific assignment or agenda waiting for you. No one can take your place in the Body of Christ. Every believer has a role to perform in building up the Kingdom of God. For the best results, please **be available**. It took a while for me to get that one. I wanted desperately to serve God earlier in my Christian life, had the scriptural background, training, wherewithal, and my fair share of trials. But for many years, I was not available due to my sinful behavior, distractions, my business goals (traveling during the Prince tour selling light-up roses, which led to opening a retail store), and one excuse after the other. It was not until after my 15-year tribulation (**1994-2009**) that I got back on track to serving the Lord with my whole heart, soul and mind.

During that period, God challenged me on abstinence, forgiving my enemies, the death of my beloved family members, my divorce, financial debt, family conflict, and deliberate instances of jealousy. It was a rude awakening, but a necessary stop in my journey which led me to a more sincere heart, a clean heart, an open heart and a forgiving heart. Don't allow past setbacks to grab hold of you and keep you behind. I am reminded of that song written by the late great Rev. Milton Brunson, "Lord, I'm Available to You." That's my prayer now, Lord, use me to show others that you are the way the truth and the life, as stated in John 14:6.

Seek to discover your spiritual gift(s) by a deeper study of the Word. You will need some private time, alone with God. Author J. E. O'Day suggests in *Discovering Your Spiritual Gifts* that you: find ways to use your spiritual gift; ask for feedback in your ministry; study a mentor; brainstorm new ideas to introduce in your faith community; and make your service to God the centerpiece of your life's purpose and planning.[1]

According to Kevin W. Earley, author of *Every Member Ministry: Spiritual Gifts and God's Design for Service,* all Christians have the responsibility to do some work for God, and that can lead to a specific ministry.[2] For 90% of people, it's telling others about Jesus; some go into ministry to become preachers, teachers, evangelists, and Christian counselors. Under the leadership of my new Pastor, I shared this book with my students when I taught a class named "Discover Your Spiritual Gift" in **2017**. The students were interested in ministry.

Author Patricia Beall Gruits provides an extensive discussion on spiritual gifts in *Understanding God and His Covenants*. She emphasizes the importance of seeking God for direction in ministry,[3] as well as using your spiritual gift to serve others.

This is summarized in 1 Timothy 4:14-16 and 2 Timothy 2:6, 15. When you accept your spiritual calling, know that it's a divine appointment that you should take seriously. You can do this through the five vocations: apostle, prophet, evangelist, pastor, and teacher as given in Ephesians 4:11-12. There are four classifications of service: elders, deacons, helps, and governments, as mentioned in 1 Corinthians 12:28. And there is a difference between a calling and a ministry.

A calling is a divine appointment for service that includes the special abilities needed for a particular ministry. When these abilities are developed by consistent exercise, they become a ministry as provided in Romans 12:6-8. Every Christian has a distinct place to fulfill in the Body of Christ. This is outlined in detail when you read 1 Corinthians 12:14-15 and 17-19. The purpose is to increase the unity and love amongst us, given our interdependence. We are not self-sufficient in the ministry of the Spirit but are perfected and completed by every other member of the Body of Christ. We need one another as we travel this lifelong journey of serving God which is provided in 1 Corinthians 12:21-25.

When you begin to explore the various ministries within your local church, you will find that there is a need for assistance, encouragement, support, and relief. In many cases, the same person has been stressed out from the overwhelming task and responsibility that comes with the territory. Perhaps no one has stepped up in a long time to offer some fresh new ideas, led by the Holy Spirit. Or, there may have been an incident where personalities have clashed and slowed down the progress within a particular ministry. Whatever the findings, make up your mind to volunteer, ask good questions, and participate on some level. It also helps to seek out the leader or director of the ministry and kindly express your desire to serve in some capacity. Speak clearly with confidence, in a non-threatening tone of voice. Relax, smile and let the Holy Spirit guide your tongue. Never bring up what you have "heard," (gossip) about the ministry, especially damaging information. People in charge can be sensitive. Make sure you tell them that God has shown you to become active in ministry, and you would like the opportunity to share your experience and serve the Lord. Take a personal inventory of your passions, skills, talents, and desire to work in ministry bringing lost souls into the Kingdom of God. Be genuine as you use your abilities to support other Christians. Let your testimony and overall behavior exhibit a level of maturity as you exemplify the fruit of the Spirit as listed in Galatians 5:22.

I want you to remember that there are many areas to choose from, depending upon the leadership of the church. This includes programs such as the youth department, missionary work, teaching in Sunday School, evangelism, marriage/family workshops, music department, and so many more. Be sincere and led by the Holy Spirit. God will direct you and reward your efforts. And stay prayerful as the process unfolds. Be open, because God may tell you to start something new. Before you know it, you'll be on the high mountain serving the Lord and saying, "He makes my feet like hinds' feet and sets me upon the high places" (Habakkuk 3:19; Psalms 18:33). To God Be the Glory! Now let your light shine.

In my personal study for discovering my spiritual gifts, I needed clarity and direction. So, my Spiritual Mother gave me a book to read called *19 Gifts of the Spirit* by Leslie B. Flynn.[4] Wow, it is still my favorite book on Spiritual Gifts! In his writing, he provides an excellent description of spiritual gifts, their role, the distribution by the Holy Spirit, and their purpose. He gives a viable approach to help you get started in ministry, serving in some capacity, and going to work for God. I really appreciated his comparative explanation of spiritual gifts, natural talents, offices in church service, and ministries. He also concludes that many believers remain unaware of their spiritual gifts for a long time, and as a result, they are not serving the Christian community. And that's why I say, it's time for you and every child of God to **Get Started With Jesus!** The world is dying and the Lord wants to enlist you.

From studying the Bible, I became fond of the ministry that God provided for the Apostle Paul. After his encounter with Jesus Christ on Damascus Road, he was sold out and totally committed to bringing Gentiles into the saving knowledge of Jesus Christ. Despite the severe persecutions as he traveled, he preached the gospel, and established churches (centers for worship) in many cities. The account of his conversion is found in the book of Acts 9:1-16.

When he heard about something going wrong in a church that was previously established, he sent a letter of concern, chastisement, challenge and correction. Much of the New Testament was written by the Apostle Paul. We call them Epistles or letters. These are the letters that were written and sent to Rome, Corinth, Ephesus, and so on. While you're learning, examine the lives of the disciples, prophets, leaders, kings, and people throughout the Word of God to get a scope of the magnitude and extreme possibilities that can manifest when your life is yielded to the call of God.

When I gained the assurance that my **spiritual gifts were teaching and exhortation,** I was in college pursuing the Liberal Arts curriculum. My intention was to major in business and eventually become a CPA. I had worked in a small business office since early in high school at age 16 and loved to do clerical work and income taxes. However, after re-dedicating my life to Jesus Christ, I decided to major in Psychology instead, and completed the studies for my Master of Arts in Guidance and Counseling. I also started working on my Doctorate Degree in Educational Psychology at Rutgers University, when living in New York City (while my husband attended law school). I completed the coursework, but not my Dissertation. After law school, we took a trip to Europe, returned to the city of Detroit, and started working in our respective careers. When the marital problems occurred, my focus and energy were zapped. I never got my Doctorate Degree.

I believed that God could use me in ministry as a Christian counselor, helping people to get saved and grow spiritually as they tackled the problems of life. I even developed a Christian Counseling program, along with my Spiritual Mother and another young counselor pursuing her Doctorate in Psychology. Yet, the idea was turned down after a few meetings, and the review by the Board of Deacons, Trustees and Insurance manager at my church. Sometimes the politics, policies, policing, or pollution of church administration can be discouraging obstacles to the work of ministry and serving God. Many young people with dreams, good ideas, new methods, and resources have abandoned the confines of traditional Christian circles due to rejection, negativity, pessimism, and disbelief in new concepts.

Yet, visionaries have to remain faithful to God and wait on Him to move on your behalf. Finally, after the marriage, career goals, shooting for success, divorce, and re-grouping, the detainment ended. I chose to trust God all over again. What I like about God is that He is Faithful. He will bring you to a place of confession, repentance, restoration, and moving forward again. Jesus is the same yesterday, today, and forever (Hebrews 13:8). He never fails!

It's so funny now, but when I think about it, I moved out of my extended, seemingly forever tribulation, right into the "favor of God." And, that is remarkable! It is proof that **you can live** your dream and serve an awesome, holy, righteous, wonderful, almighty, all-encompassing God, the Father and creator of the Universe.

I went back to Sunday School in **2008,** seeking some answers for the family issues centered around my mother's health, her age, as she was getting older and slowing down. The question was, "Who's going to be responsible and available to continue taking care of her needs?" After our father died in **1992,** I had taken the mantle to keep our family moving forward, and given the multiple circumstances, doing my best. But now, my brothers were being quite verbal, demanding, and unfair. After some heated discussions, I realized that hollering and screaming at my brothers was going to

cause me to have a heart condition, heart attack, or fall out altogether. I have never been an argumentative, mean-spirited person
and could not stand their ramblings and erratic behavior. I also
felt that their complaints and attacks were seriously wrong. But
I needed some help, clarity, direction, and relief from feeling so
stressful and disrespected.

The teacher for the class was quite knowledgeable. He was a
serious man, married with young adult children, a professional and
minister, who proclaimed the lessons with fervor and enthusiasm.
His complete presentation really motivated me to attend his class
regularly. And I did. Although I didn't know him from a personal
standpoint, I knew of him because of the fellowship amongst the
believers in the church. It's uncanny when you know that the Holy
Spirit is urging you to grow stronger in the Lord, to get it right this
time, by nudging you to use the principles that you're being taught.
I found myself accepting the challenges that he gave to the students
in his class. I began to pray for my brothers, seeking to forgive them,
provide meals when they visited, pray on their behalf, and ask God
to help me to love them again. I truly desired peace and calmness.

Every Sunday that I would attend his class, it seemed like the
Lord was always speaking to me! I never shared my personal problems with my teacher, and never once had consistent interaction
with him. However, he was the person that God was using to prick
my heart and change my soul. Finally, I decided to meet with him
and his wife, who was also active in the Youth Department at the
church. I discussed my business ideas, ministry ideas, and personal
goals. He told me to complete a study on riches from the Bible's
standpoint, stewardship and money, and suggested that I evaluate
my attitude and posture for spiritual growth in this area. It was a

healthy discussion and assignment that I still value to this day.

This particular study helped me gain some insight into my own deficiencies that were lingering around and could potentially destroy me. Interestingly enough before he died (**2010**), he provided the class with a complete outline of Sunday School lessons for continued growth in the Word of God. It was simply amazing! I am convinced that God used him to help me to get back on track to serving the Lord. I am so grateful to God for shining his light in my direction. Rest in Peace.

As I became active in the teaching ministry of our church, by serving in the New Members Class and focusing on Christian Education, I gained interest in the plans for the future direction, and development of the long-term growth for the church. Also at this time, I was asked by the First Lady to participate on the committee for Women's Day. This was very interesting because it helped me to learn about the mechanisms behind protocol, administration, programming, and planning a major church event. There are so many details that have to be considered, along with the assignments for people to carry them out. My involvement with the New Members Classes focused on teaching the basic tenets of growing in the Lord. I simply loved teaching the classes and believed that God had prepared me in this area. Starting out fresh is so important to me! And believe me, I should know! I'm convinced that if God in his majesty provides the opportunity for human beings to get their lives going in a more positive direction, then surely, they should not be ostracized, or ridiculed, made fun of, or disrespected whenever they step forward to make that decision.

In the secular world of psychological counseling and guidance, I saw that too often, the new client/patient winds up having a rough start. That first session can be very intimidating when asking the initial questions. When we had returned from New York, I was hired as an Intake Specialist at a local community mental health organization. The specific program was dedicated to serving individuals with various diagnoses, such as paranoid/schizophrenia, manic illness, depression, substance abuse, and obsessive-compulsive behaviors. They suffered with hallucinations, delusions, and other side effects from psychotropic medications. The program treated people who needed outpatient support and stability.

We worked in teams for proper case management and to develop treatment plans to monitor the clients. Unfortunately, many of these clients were "caught in the system," and the primary goal was to maintain their level of minimal function. My style of gathering the initial data was thorough, calm, and complete. I realized that the treatment, stereotypes, labels, names, misjudgments, and facts that emerge in these settings can be of concern. My caseload consisted of mentally ill, fragile, strange, and disabled persons who needed someone to listen to them. I typically never opened my clients' behavioral health records until the third or fourth session. The strategy was to have an initial, cursory view of their mental health status and current state, rather than rely solely on previous documentation of their past history. It was more important and necessary to get my own interpretation and analysis of their current condition. This was my approach to be objective in making clinical decisions as they relate to different options in therapy. By now you might be thinking, "Where is she going with this?" Well, here we go.

New Christians are like that, too! In many cases of "returning to the church and God," individuals need to be able to grow in the Lord at their own pace, with their own convictions, sprinkled with some relief from their past failures, mishaps, secret sins, disappointments, and moments of defeat! In my New Members Class, we encouraged them to complete their four classes, get baptized, be presented to the church (to receive the right hand of fellowship), and be welcomed into the membership. Some needed special prayer or the opportunity to rededicate their lives to Jesus Christ. In the classroom, they were allowed to share their anxieties, fears, and concerns as they sought God's Way to solve their problems.

Probably the largest and single-most challenging assignment of my non-singing role occurred when I was selected to be the chairperson of a major fundraiser with a good team to establish a pool of money for the future direction of the church. It was projected that these funds would be utilized to usher in the 21st Century with new technology, resources, and methods for expanding the church.

The wheels were put into motion for a Five-Year Plan (**2009 – 2014**), with the goal to raise $10,000 each year, hence $50,000. This "new money" would be kept separate from the regular church budget and operating expenses. We were fortunate and committed to raise $17,000 in 2009 and $13,000 by the end of 2010, equaling a total of $30,000.

I mentioned in an earlier chapter that the Lord allowed me to start a small business venture in **1986**, after the divorce. As a small business owner, you learn how to manage, utilize your best skills, and acquire resources for increased productivity. I had some great ideas, community contacts, proven methods, and many entrepreneurial experiences, so my mind was open to avenues of success for various ministries of the church. Change and improvement were inevitable and rapidly approaching our doors. However, in my meetings with our Senior Pastor, where I would present an update or report, he would always say, "Let me pray about it," before I could introduce a new strategy to the team and congregation. He was the type of leader who sought the Lord first before making his decisions. Overall, we had good support. In discussing the future of the church, he talked about his goal and desire for a community center, but he was certain that he "wouldn't live to see it." He was elderly, moving slower, and his health was fragile.

I was simply fascinated because, even at an old age, he still had vision! But realistically, he knew that his time was winding down for him to (as he said), "Go off the scene." I loved him dearly and learned so much from his ministry. He was kind, compassionate, a great example, and supported me throughout all my life. I am extremely grateful for his teachings. But I felt that he knew that his failing health was an issue. He reminded me of the need to embrace humility, because pride will bring me down as mentioned in Proverbs 11:2 and 16:18.

There are only three areas to guard against in the Christian life. They are the lust of the flesh, lust of the eye, and the pride of life (1 John 2:16). When he asked, I told him that mine was "**pride, being an accomplished person.**" Both of us smiled, laughed, and agreed. (**Let me just throw this in**: One year I joined the committee to assist in planning the Pastoral Anniversary at the church and the one task **he gave me, was to create the gift box,** forcing my personal lesson on humility). No, I didn't get to contact any of my friends in business, or associates in media and news to blow up the anniversary. He was a humble man and did not want the fanfare. He taught me this unforgettable lesson on **humility** and I will never forget it. I am forever grateful for the lessons I learned, which have been of great value.

Finally, one day before ending the discussion about the fundraising progress report, he shared that if anything ever happened to him, the Chairman of the Deacons would become the Official leader of the church. Ironically, I pondered and kept this information in my heart, just like Mary did in Luke 2:19, until God's time brought forth the revelation.

Despite the effectiveness and progress that we made, the vision began to wane as the health of our Senior Pastor deteriorated. It's unfortunate that the vision got dimmer. Strange things happen when a leader's vision starts to die, as stated in Proverbs 29:18. Someone must pick up the mantle, run with the baton, or carry the load to complete the task, and eventually cross the finish line. But sadly, good things only happen when God's people fervently pray as stated in James 5:16.

The fundraising plans for consideration were surprisingly delayed in **2011**. The drive was missing. Instead, the church membership voted and settled for spending the money that had been raised to remodel the church fellowship hall which had been previously named in honor of our Senior Pastor years ago. The fundraising team was told by the leadership to begin the process of obtaining quotes and resources in order to hire a contractor. The construction ideas began to circulate for this new initiative. So much for the future! It was a dismal blow.

As I recall, it was after an intense discussion during choir rehearsal in **2012**, that I personally delivered the message to the Chairman of the Deacons about leading the church. I told him that I had been made aware of this in my meetings with the Senior Pastor, who due to his illness, was getting further away from the congregation and closer to going home to live with the Lord.

The church membership was falling off on Sunday mornings, and things were beginning to rumble in the gossip circles. Mind you, all these years I continued to sing in the Senior Choir, of which I had been a member since age 18. I really cherished it, though, because that is where my Spiritual Mother had approached me one Sunday as we were changing out of our choir robes, and invited me to visit her home Bible Study. However, in church I now saw discontent on many of the faces throughout the congregation.

During this period, I stayed active with the Evangelism team, which canvassed the local neighborhood during the summer months. We took time sharing the Gospel, praying for others, passing out Bible tracts and inviting people to our church. And, finally my Christian service led me to initiate and coordinate an outreach event involving the community. It lasted for 10 years (**2005-2015**) where the gospel was preached, refreshments served, and school supplies were handed out to parents and students. It had the flavor of a great church festival in the community, where people were introduced to Jesus Christ, fed spiritually and physically, all engaged in a fun-filled atmosphere. We had a parade, Christian entertainment, a clothing giveaway, and free samples of a variety of items. You know if the people won't come inside the church, then we need to take the church to the people in the streets. We need to meet their immediate needs, share the gospel of Jesus Christ, and lead them to a better path in life! To me, that is ministry. I found my mission, was involved in ministry, and serving God.

Yet, in every Christian's life, there's always the next chapter. Towards the end of the summer in August **2011**, my dearly beloved mother died. I mustered up all of the energy that I had, to honor her life. She was a wonderful person and taught me everything that I know. Both of my parents are in heaven.

I am not going to try to describe that overwhelming feeling you get when your mother dies. But it's almost like that dropping sensation you experience when you're at the top of a roller coaster ride and you find yourself screaming all the way down. Except, instead of the ride leveling off and going around the bend to that sudden slow-down and eventual stop, you get to the drop and just linger around for a significant period of time.

You get to think deeply, feel sad, wonder about the future, all while planning the arrangements and funeral ceremony. It's different for everyone depending on the nature of the death and the bond of the relationship. I was devastated when my father died (**1992**) and doubly devastated when my mother died (**2011**). They were great parents. It was such a sad place for me because I realized that the one person who raised me, supported all of my endeavors, loved me unconditionally, and was my very own personal cheerleader throughout my entire life, was physically gone and I would never see her again in the earth. I slept on the couch for the next three months, basking in midnight tears, cherishing the memories, finalizing the family estate, and trying to think about what I was going to do next. I was shaken, sad, afraid, uncertain, and alone.

Then one day, I came to the conclusion that **I did** take care of my mother and a very good Christian sister reminded me of that fact and said, "God is going to take care of you!" I began to repeat that phrase over and over again verbally, and out loud. "I took care of my mother, and God is going to take care of me." I was holding on to that wonderful scripture deep in my heart, found in

Ephesians 6:2-3. It says, "Honor thy father and mother (which is the first commandment with promise), That it may be well with thee, and thou mayest live long on the earth." The more I said it, the more I believed it, and my faith in God was beginning to be renewed and restored. I started getting better and feeling better. I finally learned what it meant when she used to say, "Regina, you have to learn how to live one day at a time." It was all beginning to make sense to me now, as I reflected on those precious years of learning so many different lessons in life, listening to her guidance, every step of the way. She taught me to love, how to love, and how to be loved, through her words and actions. I am truly blessed because of my mother, father, and family.

Meanwhile, as the uncertainty and instability in leadership changes intensified at my local assembly, I began to assist at another small church where my dear friend was the Pastor. I wanted to get back into doing ministry and she gave me the opportunity that was helping me get through my grieving period. So I began to teach Bible classes, witness, help with their food outreach program, and learn the basics for being an armor bearer. I also shared stories during the summer day camp, and supported her after school Adult Education program.

On many Sundays, I would leave my church and go spend the rest of my afternoon fellowshipping with the small body of believers or tag along with them to attend a program at another church. It was therapeutic and refreshing, as I saw God still using me and helping me at the same time (**2011-2014**).

Several months passed and the leader of the Missions ministry at my local church inquired about purchasing polo shirts from my small business for her group. I can truly say that her request re-started my engines to get back to small business, work, and living a regular life again. It was early in **2013** that I began to associate with a group of women who represented the general mission ministries from approximately 30 local churches in the community. My impression was that they were older women, seasoned, seemingly stable, and had a heart for the things of God. I began to attend their monthly meeting to get the orders, but eventually I grew to benefit from the spiritual messages and fellowship.

It was a good turning point for me, after losing my mother, finding some joy again by serving, and now hanging around a bunch of older women who were Christians. I believe that God was moving me on to a new stage, a different chapter, a higher level of spiritual growth and development. Once again, He was training me for the higher calling. I realize now that God was putting the right people, and the right opportunities before me in order to prepare me for ministry. He was teaching me how to make the best choices that could lead to actions that would honor Him.

The Senior Pastor of our church was officially retired in **2013**, given his 50 years of Christian service (since **1963**), and the national search began for the new pastor of our local assembly. After reviewing applications, conducting interviews, evaluations, obtaining references, trial sermons, and teaching presentations, the new Pastor was finally selected, approved, and contacted to come on board as our new leader. His main objective was to renew, restore, and rebuild the value of our local church. The foundation had been laid and was in place for us to move into the 21st century. Our Senior Pastor who served faithfully for 50 years went home to be with the Lord in **2014**. I was so glad that we finally had a new Pastor in leadership; he was qualified and willing to serve in his full capacity. It was a bright, fresh, moment, at the right time for the entire church! God had smiled on us, despite the four-year gap of pastoral leadership and authority. I thought we were on our way to a new era, a new chapter in ministry. Greatness! Expectation! Fullness of Joy!

To **serve with purpose** means that you have come to the place in your relationship with God, where you **recognize and accept** your "calling" for service in Christian ministry. It is a **high calling** (Philippians 3:14). It is a **holy calling** (2 Timothy 1:9). It is a **heavenly calling** (Hebrews 3:1). You have determined to serve God with all your heart, soul, and mind as Christ himself stated in Matthew 22:37 and Mark 12:30. You realize that any and every opportunity that is presented to share the gospel of Jesus Christ is a welcome activity. You work diligently performing your job with sincerity and enthusiasm, understanding that it is an honor and privilege to serve God. Your labor is not in vain as you follow Christ. The following scriptures can enlighten and provide strength in your character: 1 Corinthians 15:58, Deuteronomy 11:13, John 12:26, and 1 Samuel 12:24. Get the Word of God deep into your spirit and allow the Holy Spirit to manifest the awesome duty of honoring God in ministry. As you serve, remember that you are working for God, and not for people. Therefore, it should be done with dedication and devotion as stated in Colossians 3:23-24 and Romans 12:11. This commitment makes you ready to spread the Word of God based on your knowledge, study, witness, and experience in trusting the risen Savior. You will find in Deuteronomy 10:12 the summation: "... serve the Lord, walk in all his ways, love him, serve the Lord with all thy heart and soul." Read Psalms 100.

As we seek to serve the Lord, it is important to forget the things of the past and reach for the future, because it is a **high calling.**

The high calling of God demands that we walk worthy of the vocation or work wherein we have been assigned. We are compelled to walk together, having the same mindset, like that song we used to sing, "Walk Together Children." We need to exercise the discipline necessary to generate results with humility, patience, and support for one another. This process is eloquently stated by Apostle Paul in Philippians 3:13-16. The high calling takes us beyond the boundaries of self-centeredness and being self-righteousness.

We lose the control of routine traditions and habits, thereby taking us into unlimited forms of intentional, on purpose, consistent Christian service and behavior that has a positive impact. This upward calling takes us above our human frailties and limitations as we depend on the power of the Holy Spirit. Your desire is to honor God. As we press towards the mark/goal for the prize of the high calling of God in Christ Jesus (Philippians 3:14), we are admonished to run the race with patience, laying aside every weight and the sin that so easily attacks us on all sides, as stated in Hebrews 12:1-2. Serve the Lord with gladness and let it go! Move forward and spread the Gospel of Jesus Christ.

Let go of the sin, the weights, the unnecessary burdens, the worries, the mess, the chains of bondage, the strongholds, the secret sins, and all those bad habits. Instead, look unto Jesus and hold your head up. You can't run any race looking down, and you can't run looking back! Make up your mind to run the Christian race looking upward, moving forward and onward, pressing toward the mark for the prize of the high calling of God in Christ Jesus! **You need to know this verse, memorize it, and get it deep down into your soul: Philippians 3:14.**

Eventually, maturity settles in and believers are drawn closer together, endeavoring to keep the unity of the Spirit in the bond of peace, as described in Ephesians 4:1-3. The high calling of God is provided in the following verses: John 15:16, Romans 8:28-30, Ephesians 1:4, 2 Thessalonians 2:13-14, 1 Peter 2:21, and 1 Corinthians 1:9.

Have you accepted the call from God in your life? Do you believe that you are chosen? The parable of the wedding feast spoken by Jesus Christ in Matthew 22:1-14 ends with, "For many are called, but few are chosen." When you take the time to study this passage of scripture, you will learn about the invitation to salvation and the necessary requirements to be a faithful disciple.

Many who have professed the Christian life will be condemned by God in the last days as pronounced in Matthew 7:21-23. That passage of scripture is significant because it points to false prophets, preachers, leaders, teachers, and those claiming to know the Lord. Jesus says that many will say (in the last days) that they did service in His name, but were actually workers of their own self-seeking sin and He will profess unto them, "I never knew you; depart from me, ye that work iniquity" (Matthew 7:23). They will not enter into the kingdom of heaven.

I love watching the Olympic runners in the relay race competitions. You get to see them running full speed ahead, with all of their energy focused on helping their team make it to the finish line in first place to be declared the winner. The only time that there is a backward motion is to hand the baton to the next runner, as he is passing by, who can hopefully keep up the pace and advance the team to win. To me, that's poetry in motion. A depiction of courage and strength.

Your goal as a leader in Christian service is to pass the baton or torch, so that God's work will continue when you're gone (if you die, get sick, or move away). We have to be willing to keep the Gospel of Jesus Christ moving forward. We live in a lost, sinful world where mankind is in need of Salvation. I cannot stress how important it is to expand and further the ministry of Jesus Christ on all levels. If we followed the examples in the Holy Bible, there is a method to guide our steps. God **always had the next person in line** to take the lead in a decent, orderly fashion with dignity and respect, according to His Will. When you review the lives of Abraham, Isaac, Jacob, Noah, Moses, Joshua, King David, Joseph, Daniel, and so many other prophets, kings, and leaders, God always had the next successor. When we trust God and follow His guidance, we would obtain better results when transition is taking place.

And, Jesus is coming back soon as stated in 1 Thessalonians 4:13-18. Just look around at the horrible condition of this entire world! Everywhere there is sin!

I wrote this in 2020 during a **Global Pandemic.** Daily protests were happening throughout our nation and abroad for racial injustices and police brutality in the Black community. The economic outlook for people became bleak, with millions seeking unemployment benefits. Government officials in many countries closed their borders due to a new virus without a cure which has infected nearly 212 million people and claimed more than 4.4 million lives around the world as of August 2021.

The pandemic caused volatility in the financial markets, at some points causing crashes without any foreseeable relief or remedy. And the healthcare industry was besieged with unprecedented challenges in caring for patients. The political systems were rife with chaos, confusion, mixed opinions, inconsistent messages, uncertainty, doubt, constant fear, and conflicting information with regard to tackling these crises. Coupled with the racial division due to police brutality against Blacks, which is affecting mankind, the overall state of the mental, physical, emotional, financial, educational, and social well-being of the family unit has been weakened and is diminishing every day.

The pandemic caused a dreadful time in history as people tried to guard against the coronavirus and stay safe by using masks and gloves as personal protective equipment. And if that were not enough to swallow, we were mandated to embrace this brand-new concept and phenomenon called "social distancing" to stay healthy. Social interaction decreased in public settings, businesses closed, and visiting others was mostly eliminated. We were in a dismal state facing sickness, death, and funerals without family members present to say goodbye.

The fear and grief of the deadly pandemic amplified the fact that it is time to make a change in your life. It's time to rethink the journey that you have been on, and check your disposition toward God. I personally believe that we're running out of time, wasting time, and spending too much time on routine habits associated with "just going to church." The need has come for **Prayer** to be the most important and common denominator that every person embraces in today's society.

People are dying every day, regardless of age, socioeconomic status, ethnic group, personal background, financial position, or physical health condition. We all need a closer walk with God.

We aim to serve the Lord with gladness (Psalms 100:2) because it is **a holy calling.** When you serve with purpose, you realize that God, the father, is strictly business! It is a serious place of responsibility, one that cannot be taken for granted. He sets the bar high as explained in 1 Peter 1:13-16, where we are told to gird up the loins of our minds, be sober, and be obedient children of God. We are expected to relinquish ourselves from the foolishness of our former lusts, and to maintain a holy lifestyle. Here's where most people will turn a deaf ear and reject this truth and exclaim, "I lose you," as my very own Pastor would say. But it specifically says in verse 16, "But as it is written, Be ye holy; for I am holy." We must come out of the world to live a lifestyle that is pleasing and acceptable to God. We are supposed to live our lives according to His standards.

It is all recorded in His Word, and to be holy, we first must acknowledge this fact and follow His instructions. If you try to function in your own strength, with a personal agenda, you will lose a lot of ground, fall behind and possibly deteriorate. Efforts to serve while seeking the approval of your peers, showing a charismatic personality, or flashing a significant knowledge of the scriptures, will be to your detriment, and shamefully exposed when you least expect it! Then we must take our daily dose to be filled with the Holy Spirit, in order to live up to these standards, as mentioned in Ephesians 5:17-21. We are advised to be clothed with humility, knowing that God resists the proud, but gives grace to the humble. As we humble ourselves under his mighty hand, He will exalt us in due time (1 Peter 5:5-6). Not my will, but God's will at the right time in my life, under the right circumstances, with the right people, for the right reasons, which glorify Him.

Finally, the holy calling forces committed believers to "**stand out**" from the crowd. There is no doubt that God is very concerned about holiness. When you review the description in 1 Peter 2:9-10,

He states that we are a "chosen generation, a royal priesthood, a holy nation, a peculiar people, called out of darkness into his marvelous light, and now are called the people of God who have obtained his mercy." Hallelujah! Thank you, Jesus! We no longer walk in darkness living a life of sin, or half-hearted commitment, or a life full of doubt, fear, and unbelief. Instead, we are really special—children of God with a mission, purpose, and desire to serve the Lord and build up the Kingdom of God. This is why in 2 Peter 1:10, we are told to be diligent to make our calling and election sure, as partakers of the divine nature, which is given unto us, according to the divine power of our Savior, Jesus Christ.

As we come to the conclusion of serving the Lord with purpose, we cannot leave out the significance of the heavenly calling. It is **a heavenly calling** in God where He ordains us and sends us out to save lost souls. The heavenly calling is by God, from God, for God, and through the mercy of God to utilize mankind to live according to the image in which he created us. Both male and female were created in the image of God as found in Genesis 1:26-27.

In Hebrews 3:1, the scripture states, "Wherefore, holy brethren, partakers of the heavenly calling, consider the Apostle and High Priest of our profession, Christ Jesus." When you come to the place of surrendering your life and accepting Jesus Christ as your Lord and Savior, the power of the Holy Spirit begins to work on dispelling sin from your old standard of living.

At a certain point in your growth in the Lord, you will make the ultimate decision (one way or another), to serve the Lord. That is when you realize that you are ready to lead people to God, or back to God, or to trust God, once again. It is an awesome responsibility with extreme benefits and blessings. My Spiritual Mother said, "In order to be used by God, you must have a burden for people." Now, let me give you an imaginary example. The Holy Spirit goes ahead of us, and touches the life of some lost soul. That person who is in dire straits has multiple problems which they cannot solve. Somehow, somewhere, and at the appointed time, you will meet them along life's journey, and they're primed and ready to seek God for His answers to their problems. God then allows a verbal exchange to occur, and the plan of Salvation is presented to that person.

The result is a precious seed that is planted within the heart of that lonely individual who just might accept Jesus Christ, or at least have come to a better understanding of approaching God's throne of Grace. Either way, the outcome is God's business. He already knows the depth of that interaction and its impact upon that person's life. This divine intervention is ordained by God, from God, and for the purpose of God. The approach, contact, and execution were designed by God.

The heavenly calling is not a political election, nor popularity contest. It's not even based upon your personal accomplishments such as wealth, education, fame, or good fortune. It is, in fact, pre-announced, predestined, and pre-ordained by a holy, righteous Almighty God, who works mightily through his infinite power in the life of an ordinary person (I love that 1977 song, "Just Ordinary People, God Uses Ordinary People," by Danniebelle Hall).

However, **You make** the choice. You see, God detects the true heart of a believer, and God selects or chooses them. After the decision to follow Him is made, then He sets them apart and elects them for Godly service. At a specific time, which is determined by God, He launches them into the Christian arena filled with the

Holy Spirit and armed with the whole armor of God. The power of the Holy Spirit then catapults that individual believer into a number of religious settings. And they are used by God to alter the trajectory of battered, suffering, and hurt populations where the Gospel of Jesus Christ is so desperately needed. That is what I call divine intervention. However, you do make the choice.

God chose us before the foundation of the world and predestined us to be a child of God through our acceptance and identification with our Lord and Savior (Ephesians 1:4-6). We have redemption through his blood, the forgiveness of sins, the mystery of his will. We have also obtained an inheritance, and we are sealed by the Holy Spirit (Ephesians 1:7-14). We are the adopted sons and daughters of God, the moment we receive Jesus Christ (Galatians 3:25-26, 4:4-7; 1 John 3:1-2). There is a secret place of the Most High and it is wonderful to abide under the shadow of the Almighty. He is my refuge (Psalms 91:1-16).

Furthermore, the Apostle Paul tells Timothy, his son in the faith, that he is thankful to Jesus Christ that the gospel was committed to his trust and put into his hands to share with others. He's thankful that God had mercy on him, counted him faithful, and planted him into the ministry as stated in 1 Timothy 1:11-12.

It was God who elected him, straightened out his life, gave the new orders, put him in business, put him on the map, so to speak, and he faithfully served the Lord.

There is another Apostle who walked with Jesus Christ, named Peter, who addresses the elect according to the foreknowledge of God, in discussing trials and suffering (1 Peter 1:1-3, 6-14, 2:20-21, 4:1-2, 12-13, 16-19). He then sums it up by stating after the suffering, you'll come out mature, stable, strengthened and settled (1

135

Peter 5:10). He goes on to admonish us to give diligence to make sure our calling and election are sure to prevent falling away from trusting God. We should add the following great Christian virtues to our lifestyle: giving all diligence, while adding to your faith, virtue, knowledge, self-control, patience, godliness, brotherly kindness, and love (2 Peter 1:3-8;10). This life-long journey is God's business, especially when you serve the Lord. You gain purpose and authority.

To serve with purpose is **a high calling, a holy calling, and a heavenly calling.** As you grow in your relationship with God, you become a true vessel to proclaim the gospel. We are a holy people, a special people, and above all, people chosen by God for a specific objective (Deuteronomy 7:6; Ephesians 1:4; 1 Peter 1:2). This election is not based upon our human merit, but solely given by the Grace of God (Romans 9:11, 11:5-6; Ephesians 2:8-10).

Lastly, the election is from the divine will of God through Jesus Christ, who said, "You have not chosen me, but I have chosen you, and ordained you, that you should go and bring forth fruit, and that your fruit should remain; that whatever ye shall ask of the Father in my name, he may give it to you" (John 15:16). Here is the illumination: God is sovereign, and He chooses whom he will use for his glory, and who is chosen for distinct services. (Luke 6:13; Acts 9:15; 1 Corinthians 1:27-28; John 15:19). Election means **chosen or to choose** as set forth in Deuteronomy 7:6, 1 Peter 5:13, and 2 Peter 1:10, written in the Old Testament and the New Testament.

Therefore, as we grow in grace and knowledge of our Lord and Savior Jesus Christ as stated in 2 Peter 3:18, we should walk worthy of the vocation to which we are called as given in Ephesians 4:1. The Holy Bible tells us exactly how to walk. We are to walk uprightly, walk at liberty, walk with integrity, walk wisely, walk in the light of the Lord, walk together, walk humbly, walk in newness of life, walk not after the flesh, walk by faith, walk circumspectly, walk worthy of the Lord, walk honestly, and to walk in the light (Psalms 26:11, 56:13; Proverbs 10:9, 28:18; Psalms 84:11, 119:45; Proverbs 19:1, 28:6, 26; Isaiah 2:5; Amos 3:3; Micah 6:8; Romans 6:4, 8:1; 2 Corinthians 5:7; Ephesians 4:1, 5:15; Colossians 1:10; 1 Thessalonians 2:12, 4:1, 12; 1 John 1:7).

We should walk in the fear and admonition of the Lord, serving wholeheartedly.

Yes, my dear friend, this is the time. You have got to get this and start growing closer to God. Grow in the Word of God. Grow up from past hurt and pain. Grow out of bad habits and strongholds. And grow through your personal trials, setbacks, and tribulations. Cast all your cares on him and trust in the Lord. (Peter 5:7-9; Ephesians 4:14-15; Proverbs 3:5-6).

When we follow Him, every spirit-filled believer, leader in ministry, servant of the gospel, and child of God should remember and proclaim the following words: "The Spirit of the Lord God is upon me, because the Lord has anointed me to preach good tidings unto the meek; he has sent me to bind up the brokenhearted, to proclaim liberty to the captives, and the opening of the prison to them that are bound" (Isaiah 61:1).

Also remember that, "The Spirit of the Lord is upon me, because he has anointed me to preach the gospel to the poor; he has sent me to heal the brokenhearted, to preach deliverance to the captives, and recovering of sight to the blind, to set liberty them that are bruised; to preach the acceptable year of the Lord" (Jesus). The prophet stated this in Isaiah 61:1 (Old Testament) and Jesus Christ said it in Luke 4:18-19 (New Testament), respectively. When this is done, the gospel will continue to go forth, sinners will be saved, fulfilling the Great Commission.

Serving with purpose is where I am in my relationship with God, and the outgrowth of this book correlates with my assignment as the lead teacher of our New Members Ministry at my local church. The Lord has blessed me with a teaching, giving, singing, and counseling ministry. I simply love every minute of serving the Lord.

I give Him all the glory for effectuating change in my life. He is my Redeemer, Provider, and Sustainer. I have direction and the Peace of God every day.

Conclusion

After all that has been said, there is still one critical question. Where are **YOU** in your relationship with God? Or, if you're already a born-again believer of Jesus Christ, will **you** answer the call? Will you decide to serve, to give, to follow God and allow his authority to resonate in your life? This is the task at hand. The time is now for you to get started with Jesus!

Perhaps you have come to a better understanding of the Christian journey and want to get started, grow closer, or re-dedicate your life to God. That is the purpose of this book. My goal is to help you gain strength and grow to develop the level of spiritual maturity that pleases God. Let me explain it in an easier way. The Bible describes three categories of man and you fall within one of them.

The Spiritual Man is saved and growing in Christian maturity (Ephesians 4:17-29). The Carnal Man is saved, but worldly and immature in the things and knowledge of God (1 Corinthians 3:1-3; Romans 8:5-8). And, The Natural Man is a sinner, unsaved, and does not know the things of God (Romans 3:23; 1 Corinthians 2:14). Which category represents you?

There is a big difference between living a life that is totally yielded to the Holy Spirit, and a life that goes to church Sunday after Sunday without any spiritual fulfillment. The Christian Life is an on-growing process until you finish your time here on Earth. This is the pathway that leads to Spiritual Growth and Maturity and walking fervently in the Will of God. The choice is yours!

Thank you for taking the time and energy to read this material. May the Grace of God encompass your life and the Peace of God keep your heart and mind throughout your Christian journey.

The Lessons in the Appendix will inspire and help you to grow closer to God.

Be Peaceful,

Regina A. DuBose

Photo Gallery
Section 2

My paternal grandparents: **Mary Lou Neal married William Felix Hinkle** and created **the Hinkle family.**

My first cousins, Jackie, Vernice, Rufus, and Dr. Shelley, are with my **"Aunt Toot"** (Ruth Miller, my mom's sister), who taught me how to make **those delicious sweet potato pies!**

My first cousin **Gloria Jean Wesson** was close to our family. Her adult children: **Dwight, Steven, Byron, Denise, & Freida.**

Studying the Word of God was one of the best times of my life. We were learning, hearing, and growing strong to do the work of the Lord!

Bible Study at my Spiritual Mother's home was motivating and challenging; the place where **"The Fellowship"** was established. **Sharon, Stephanie, Karen, and Revoydia** are in a session.

After much prayer and discussion, we agreed to allow men to join our Bible Study. Here is Margo and Robert sharing information about a specific subject.

Members of "The Fellowship," Dionne, Carmen, Tanya, Karen, & Revoydia lift their hands to praise God at a Christian Retreat in 1976.

Our signature jumpsuits.

Great choreography and routines.

In **1973**, I became a member of **"The Versatilities,"** a talented singing group that performed locally throughout Metro Detroit in our unique, colorful jumpsuits. Our stage appearance, vocals, and dramatic skits entertained and educated our audiences. **Members: Debra, Kathryn, Lynnette, Vanessa, Cynthia, myself, and Gwen (not pictured)**. We had fun singing, dancing, and acting while reaching for the stars in the music industry.

I'm leading this song in my own style.

In 1973 we performed, **"Neither One of Us," at Cass Technical High School Talent Show.** It was a big hit and the crowd went crazy as Debra was the lead singer!

And here she is! The lady with the big voice who sang, **"How Big Is God?"** I was 10 years old when I first heard that song. She is surrounded by church members and friends, and taught many young people to sing to the Glory of God. **I will always cherish her legacy. Thank you, Mrs. Elizabeth Davis.**

The concert by **Morgan State University Choir in 2003** was an exuberating performance of choral music excellence under the direction of the late, great **Dr. Nathan M. Carter**. I took a moment to praise God for his goodness and mercy in my life.

I am standing with two musical geniuses who influenced me and my daughter: **Dr. Dorgan J. Needom**, Minister of Music at Unity Baptist Church; and **Dr. Nathan M. Carter**, Choral Music Director at Morgan State University.

Sequina celebrates with her father and brother, Michael, after graduating from Morgan State University in 2003.

Marsha came to support our **Harvest Festival in 2009.** I was a Chairperson.

Rev. Dr. Nathan Johnson, Pastor of Tabernacle Missionary Baptist Church was the guest speaker for our **Harvest Festival in November 2009.** I am standing with **Rev. Dr. Valmon D. Stotts, Pastor of Unity Missionary Baptist Church.**

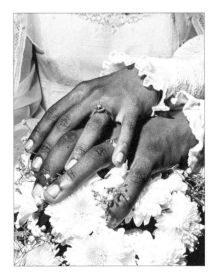

On **August 19, 1978,** my high school sweetheart married me, and we became **Mr. & Mrs. Sequoia and Regina DuBose.**

Our wedding ceremony and marriage were a beautiful exchange of love and affection. It was a special time in our lives that we will never forget.

He loved me and I loved him.

Our wedding party consisted of family, friends, and members from the Fellowship.

Our parents shared with us on this wonderful day.

We were a happy couple and enjoyed life to its fullest as we navigated through marriage, college, graduate and law school, and the joy of parenting.

We were blessed with our child, Sequina Bianca DuBose, born on August 18, 1980, the first day of law school in **New York City.**

* **Sequina Bianca DuBose** *

Children are a blessing from God and she brought so much joy into our lives. Psalm 127

Our bouncing baby girl at one and two years old.

152

After the divorce in 1986, my faith in God, focus, and fortitude keep me moving forward. I started a small business called, **"The Alexis Company."**

I wound up with a concussion and a fractured pelvis, and the vehicle was totaled, during this horrible accident **in July 1998, but God spared my life.**

Proud parents who are truly blessed, supporting our precious daughter at her performance.

New members were eager to join Unity Baptist Church under the leadership of Pastor Lee C. Winfrey (**2015-2018**).

I served in the **New Members Ministry** along with Gerry, Jackie, Gloria, Marva, Valerie, Dr. DaNita, and Mrs. Berry. I also participated in the **Evangelism Ministry at Unity Baptist Church.**

Here am I, fervently teaching the **New Members Class** in the sanctuary at Partakers Church on October 28, 2018. I really appreciate the preaching, teaching, and leadership of **Rev. Dr. Lee C. Winfrey and his wife Kimberly at Partakers Church Baptist in Detroit.** Earlier in July 2018, my daughter Sequina attended our Women's Day program and sang a beautiful solo. My soul was stirred to honor and praise God!

My Christian journey has come full circle. From singing as a gospel recording artist (**1989-1991**), to teacher, to counselor, then serving in evangelism and learning to give to the Kingdom of God.

I sang on a program during the **NAACP Convention** held in Detroit, Michigan during July 2007. **Ms. Eunice Wade** was my accompanist—a great songwriter, choir director, and colleague in Music Ministry.

I am grateful to God for all of my teachers.

In **1968**, I met and was baptized by **Rev. Valmon D. Stotts** at Unity Baptist Church. He attended the Harvest Festival in **2009**. Thank you, Lord.

I met my first boss, **Mr. James R. Thompson, CPA in 1972**. He came to the 10th Anniversary of my small business in **1996**. Thank you, Lord.

I was astonished to see my **sixth grade** teacher, **Mrs. Jacquetta Crews, at Linda Moragne's** event in **2019**. Thank you, Lord.

Special thanks to my Chairpersons who supported and directed the vision of my 35th Anniversary Celebration and Book Release. You are appreciated for your amazing talent, insight, knowledge, consideration, and organizational skills. I am truly blessed and grateful to God that you are my team. I love you all.

Dr. DaNita Weddle Chairperson

Mr. Arthur Williams, Program Chairperson, and Ms. Sheri Burton, Marketing/Sales Chairperson

Appendix

Getting Started with Jesus

YOUR RELATIONSHIP WITH GOD starts the moment you accept Jesus Christ as your personal Lord and Savior. But let's face it. Just like any other human relationship, it must grow, be cultivated, and blossom into something meaningful. That requires spending time to get to know God, His Will, His Word, and His Way. It takes some commitment. In this section, I have provided 12 brief lessons that represent a model for Godly, Christian living in a wicked, evil, demonic world that is heavily influenced by Satan. They are essential for developing a formula to stay on track as you build a consistent pattern for your spiritual growth and maturity.

LESSON ONE— THE OVERVIEW— Make a decision to accept Jesus Christ as your Lord and Savior and build a relationship with Him. This entails learning all about Him (who, what, when, where, why, and how). You must spend time studying, reading, praying, and meditating on the Word of God. God loves you and cares about your life. We are born into sin. Christ died for our sin and He is the Only way to God. Read Romans 3:23 and 6:23, John 3:16-17, Ephesians 2:8-9, Romans 10:9,10, 1 Corinthians 5:17, and

Revelation 3:20 and memorize them (use notes, 3x5 cards, etc.). Read St. John in the Holy Bible (KJV), New Testament.

LESSON TWO— THE HOLY BIBLE— Commit to spend time with God every day. Find a quiet place in your environment for time to read the Word. Mine is early in the morning before I start my day. The Holy Bible is the primary tool for God to communicate to you. He speaks through his Word. You talk with Him through prayer. There are 66 books in the Bible, divided in two sections: Old Testament and New Testament. All scripture was written by men inspired by God. The Word is sharp and revealing. The Bible provides stories that relate to your life concerns, and the answers to live according to God's standards and wisdom. Read 2 Timothy 2:15 and 3:16-17, Psalms 119:9-11, Hebrews 4:12, and Psalms 19:7-14.

LESSON THREE—THE CREATION—The creation of the earth and mankind is recorded in Genesis Chapter 1-2:3. Everything was created by God and it was all good. On the seventh day He rested. Man was told to be fruitful, multiply, and have dominion over every living thing. Read and memorize Genesis 1:1, 26-28, 2:1-3, and 2:21-24, Psalms 24, and John 1:1. The world was a paradise.

LESSON FOUR—THE FALL OF MAN—The Fall of Man led to chaos, confusion, curses, and conflict, and is written in Genesis 3:1-24. The introduction, influence, and impact of Sin on God's creation was due to one act of disobedience; and created the need for a "blood sacrifice" to redeem mankind. All attempts by man failed from Adam to the Jewish Nation to Judges, and Kings. Many laws were broken as well as The Ten Commandments. Do an extensive study of Genesis 11-50 to learn the history of Abraham, Isaac, and Jacob. Read Genesis 3:1-24 and Exodus 1-20, and memorize Genesis 2:23-24, 3:6-7, and 3:14-24. Understand how sin took control.

LESSON FIVE—JESUS CHRIST, THE GREAT PROVISION— Jesus is the great provision for the sins of the world. His virgin birth, walk on earth as a boy, his occupation, the miracles that he performed during his ministry, the sermon on the mount, and the call of the disciples (fishermen) are recorded in the four Gospels of the New Testament: Matthew, Mark, Luke, and John. His death, burial and resurrection paid the price for the entire world to bring us back to God. Read and study each Gospel and memorize key verses: Matthew 5:16, 6:9-18, and 28:16-20, Mark 4:1-20 and 11:20-24, Luke 2:8-14 and 22:7-46, John 1:1, 1;12, 1:14, 14:6, and 16:24. Make notes as you gain knowledge about our Lord and Savior.

LESSON SIX—THE POWER OF PRAYER—Develop a meaningful prayer life. We are commanded to pray. Learn the Lord's Prayer. Pray in the Name of Jesus and revere God through prayer. Sin will delay answers to your prayers. Focus on ACTS—Adoration, Confession, Thanksgiving, and Supplication. Pray for your fellow man, those in authority, and the Kingdom of God. Read and memorize Luke 18:1, Matthew 26:41, Isaiah 55:6, 1 Thessalonians 5:17-18, and 1 Timothy 2:1-3.

LESSON SEVEN—THE BAPTIST DOCTRINE—Learn the reason for Baptism and Holy Communion. Understand the symbolic representation of the bread and wine. Know the importance of examining your actions before taking Communion.

Read about John the Baptist, the Last Supper, and the Crucifixion of Jesus Christ. Take time to study Matthew 3:1-11, 12-17, and 26:26-29, Luke 22:14-20, John 3:22-36, and 1 Corinthians 10:16-22 and 11:23-30. Learn by studying.

LESSON EIGHT—PERSONAL STEWARDSHIP—It is God's Will and for Christians to be faithful and wise stewards over everything that He has given to us. This includes, our time, talent, treasure, things, tissue (body), tongue, temperament (attitude and behavior), and giving. Discover and cultivate your spiritual gift to serve God in come capacity. Read Matthew 25:14-30 and Luke 12:41-48. Examine the proper use of money and learn to improve your stewardship in all areas of your life. Read and memorize Malachi 3:7-12, 1 Timothy 6:10, Luke 6:38, Ephesians 4:7-12 and 29, 1 Corinthians 6:13-20 and 10:11-14, Philippians 2:5-11 and 8-9, Isaiah 43:7, James 3:5-10, 2 Corinthians 6:11-18, and Hebrews 13: 20-21.

LESSON NINE—BEWARE OF SIN—The characteristics of sin can prevent a faithful, fruitful, fulfilling walk in the Christian life. Learn the differences between transgressions, iniquity, trespasses, breaking the law, and sin which all represent disobeying, disregarding, and denouncing God. Read and memorize Deuteronomy 9:7, Proverbs 24:9, James 1:13-15 and 4:17, 1 John 3:4, 8, and 5:17, Psalms 66:18, Isaiah 53:5-6 and 59:1-15, and 2 Peter 2:6-8.

Read and study the remedy for temptation in 1 Corinthians 10:13, Colossians 3:5-6, 1 Peter 5:8-9, and 1 Corinthians 10:5-9, 14. Be aware of sin and your surroundings. Stay very alert.

LESSON TEN—THREE CATEGORIES OF MAN—Read, meditate, study, and memorize scripture that discusses "the fear of the Lord." Describe the Natural, Carnal, and Spiritual Man according to scripture. Study the parable of the Sower and how it relates to growing spiritually versus falling away from the truth of God. Compare and contrast the path of the seeds that fall by the wayside, on stony ground, on thorny ground, and on good ground. Read Proverbs 1:7, 3:7, and 14:7, Psalms 19:9, Job 28:28, and Luke 1:50. Read Mark 4:1-25, Matthew 13:1-23, and Luke 8:4-15. Read and memorize 1 Corinthians 2:12-14, Ephesians 2:1-3, 1 Peter 2:1-3, 1 Corinthians 3:1-3, and Romans 8:5-8. Also read and memorize Galatians 5:1, Colossians 1:10 and 3:1-3, Hebrews 12:1-2, Ephesians 2:8-9 and 6:10-18, and 2 Peter 3:1. This lesson will open your eyes to good fruit.

LESSON ELEVEN—WATCH YOUR APPETITE—Be encouraged in your faith and walk according to God's standard. Study and learn what to "ingest" and what type of spiritual "food" to eat. Jesus is the bread of life. His bread satisfies every hunger and pain—physically, emotionally, socially, and psychologically. Read Isaiah 6:5-8, Jeremiah 1:4-10, and John 6:35, 48 and 51. Love the Lord with your whole heart; Matthew 22:37-40. Do the Word of God; James 1:22-25 and Matthew 7:21. Desire the milk to grow: 1 Peter 2:2 and Hebrews 5:12-14. Prepare to eat meat: Hebrews 5:12-14 and Romans 14:11-21. Put on Godly behaviors and put off the world's standards (i.e., cable, tv, secular radio/programs, news, gossip, lust). Read and memorize Ephesians 6:11, 1 John 1:9, Colossians 2:2-8 and 3:1-14, 1 Peter 4:7, and Romans 12:1-2. Renew your mind, change your habits, stretch with Jesus!

LESSON TWELVE—THE RISEN SAVIOR—Jesus Christ is the Savior of the world. He is the only way to God. His suffering, death, burial, and resurrection is recorded in the Holy scriptures. Read, study, and meditate on Isaiah 53:4-7, Psalms 22, Mark 16:1-7 and 16-23, and John 20:1-18 and 14:6. There is power in the Name of Jesus; John 16:24, Philippians 2:5-11, and Romans 10: 9,10. Jesus is the great I am: John 8:58, and Revelation 1:8 and 17:18. He sent the Comforter, the Holy Spirit to live in us, teach, and guide us until He returns; Acts 1:3-11, John 14:13-21, and Thessalonians 4:14-17. He's coming back, again.

These lessons are designed to strengthen your relationship with God. Salvation comes through prayer. You simply ask—out loud—for Jesus to come into your heart and believe that God raised Him from the dead as stated Romans 10:9-10. He stands at the door of your heart: Revelation 3:20. Get started, renew, or restore your life with Jesus Christ: John 3:16-17.

You can pray this prayer right now: Lord Jesus, please come into my heart. I accept you as my Lord and Savior. I believe that your death, burial, and resurrection paid the penalty for my sins. Thank you, Lord, for saving me and giving eternal life. Then, connect with a local church, and live for Jesus Christ.

God bless you.

Author Bio

REGINA DUBOSE WAS BORN in Detroit, Michigan in 1957. She was educated in the Detroit Public School system and was raised in a loving family with her parents and four brothers. In 1968, her parents joined a local Baptist church and began to instill a love of God and spiritual teachings into their children. Regina became a member of the church when she was 10 years old, after professing to believe in Jesus Christ. She became active in Sunday School and was a member of the Children's Choir. At 18 years old, she became the youngest person to join the church's Senior Choir. In that same year, her life changed when through the encouragement of her spiritual mentor she decided to re-dedicate her life to Christ.

Regina received a Bachelor of Arts degree in Psychology and a Master of Arts degree in Guidance and Counseling from Wayne State University, with continued graduate studies at Rutgers University. For 13 years, she was a professional counselor in the community mental health field and gerontology focusing on education, support, treatment plans, and stabilizing mental health clients.

Regina's biblical training, combined with her background in psychology and counseling, has enhanced her ability to examine human behavior while viewing challenges through a spiritually-guided lens. Regina actively serves in her home church Partakers Church Baptist under the leadership of Rev. Dr. Lee C. Winfrey, Sr. She serves as a member of the Board of Christian Education, the Lead Teacher for the New Members Classes, the Choir President, and as a member of the Women's Ministry.

Regina's favorite scripture is Philippians 4:13, "I can do all things through Christ who strengthens me." She strongly believes that peace comes from maintaining a personal relationship with God. She shares her life with her daughter, Dr. Sequina DuBose, who is a classical musician, opera singer, and college professor. Regina loves to travel, cook, sing, and play board games to relax.

In *Getting Started With Jesus*, Regina provides the methods by which she has approached many of life's challenges and encourages readers to move toward true spiritual growth and maturity.

Acknowledgments

I THANK THE SOVEREIGN Will of God who ordered my steps throughout my journey as a Christian woman, while orchestrating the scenes in my life that created this book. I thank my African Ancestors who made it across the Atlantic Ocean to America.

I thank Mary Lou Neal and William Felix Hinkle, my paternal grandparents who created the Hinkle family. I thank Bessie Moor and David Creag, who were my maternal grandparents and created my mother Rosie Lee, who married Samuel Matthew Hinkle. I thank my loving parents for love and kindness. I thank my brothers Samuel M. Hinkle, Jr. and James Allen Hinkle for your brilliance. I thank all of my Aunts, Uncles, and Cousins who were around during my childhood upbringing.

Thank you, Aunt Harrietta (Cousin Jr. Ruffin), Uncle Harry (Cousin Helen), Aunt Nancy and Uncle George Manuel (Cousin Victor), Aunt Littie Ann (who lived with us), Mary (Dear) Freeman and Uncle Sylvester, Mama Freeman and Alexis Jane and Donald Hill (my first cousin whom I was named after). I thank Cousin Mary Catherine Mason who owned a restaurant in Dayton, Ohio. I also thank Aunt Mary Cooper and Uncle Eddie (Cousin Billy Bo), Aunt Ruth (Toot) Miller and Uncle Rufus (Rufus James), and Uncle Robert Lee Creag (who lived with us).

I thank Mary and Auntre DuBose, my mother and father in law who showed me kindness and love (Sequoia), and James R. Thompson, CPA (my first boss). I thank Mr. Will Burnett (WB) Sanders (my dad's best friend), and Rev. Dr. Valmon D. Stotts (Pastor), Mrs. Dorothy Griffin and Mrs. Annie Ellis (my Sunday School teachers).

It is with great appreciation and in loving memory that I acknowledge your presence in the early years of my life. You are truly missed; I thank God for your contribution to my personal journey.

I thank all of my relatives, young people, neighbors, church members, students, and friends who brought about personal challenge and growth in my life. I thank my brothers Ronald Edwin and William Dwayne Hinkle for your love. I thank Carolyn, Janice, Marsha Lorraine, Giselle, and Marsha Hinkle for your kindness.

I thank my best friends from high school: Mrs. Yasmin Atkins and Dr. Pamela Bradford; Jaunice Flowers; Mrs. Joyce Keener and the Super Bowl Clan; Vincent and the Goree family; as well as Nina R. Scott and Patrice DeBose (Renaissance High School Varsity Chorus). I thank Marlene Archey Crim, Esq. for your words of wisdom. Thank you, Dr. Irma Hamilton, teachers, and educators. I thank my partner, graphics designer, and friend Mr. Arthur Williams and his wife Shanell, and Mary Johnson Grant (Cousin Mae Mae) for pushing me forward to reach my goals. I thank my first cousins Floyd Johnson and Gloria Jean Wesson, who showered me with love and affection. I thank the Trios of older women (Titus 2:3-5) who were my role models: Zeborah Hampton Hardy, Denise Livingston Dryden, and Shelley Peters Davis (neighbors); Vernice Miller, Dr. Shelley McIntosh, and Jacqueline Miller (first cousins on my mother's side); Jewel Jones, Nancy Mayes, and Mary Johnson Grant (first cousins on my father's side); and Mrs. Rose Harvey, Mrs. Elizabeth Davis, and Mrs. Sarah Jenkins (great church soloists). I sincerely thank Mrs. Jacquetta Crews, my sixth grade teacher who also taught my daughter, and all of the great teachers who were at Hanneman Elementary School, especially during the 1960s.

Thank all of you for your special role in the development of my character, education, leadership, strength, fortitude and courage as a Christian woman.

I thank Eric J. Bowren, CPA of Edwards, Ellis & Associates, P.C. Thank you for financial intelligence, administration, and consultation. I thank Dr. Sequina DuBose and Mr. Ajani Winston for technical genius, graphic design, and personal assistance. I thank my mentor, Dr. Glenda Price, who steered me in the right direction with wisdom, knowledge, and inspiration. Thank you for embracing my vision. Thank you, Sheri Burton, President of Midwest Civic Council of Block Clubs, for believing and compelling me to walk; I can now run. Thank you, Robert Quinn Hampton, for your sincere dedication and commitment over the years.

I want to thank the religious institutions, programs, churches and ministries that I was exposed to which provided training and mastery in Christian principles, facts, values, doctrine, instruction, gospel music, ministry, leadership, and evangelism.

I thank the spiritual leadership and pastoral counseling of Rev. Dr. Valmon D. and Ethel Stotts. Thank you Rev. Robert and Audrey Royal for allowing me to teach at the Youth Retreat. I thank my Sunday School teachers Rev. Johnnie Byrd, Rev. Dempsey and Sandra Harrison, Patricia and Mike Sherman (my team teachers), and Rev. Ed and Valerie Morgan. I thank Mrs. Eunice Wade for being my friend, music arranger, adviser, composer, and accompanist. I thank Dr. Dorgan J. Needom, Minister of Music, for musical excellence in the church community, and the entire music department; thank you choir members, congregation, colleagues, and friends at Unity Baptist Church located in Detroit, Michigan.

I thank Dr. Pamela Bradford for inviting me to teach on Teenage Dating and Abstinence to the youth at New Calvary Baptist Church. Thank you Rev. Haman and Malettor Cross whose Detroit's Afro American Mission was a Biblical training center. I thank Pastor Angela L. Stallworth of Crown of Glory International Ministries, for allowing me to serve in her ministry. You taught me to persevere during transition, trust God when miserable, perform the duties of an armor bearer, and help to expand my capacity. I thank the different teachers who provided lessons in various Bible courses through the programs of Metropolitan District Congress of Christian Education (MEDCCE), Women's Auxiliary, National Baptist Congress of Christian Education, Detroit Bible College, and the Wolverine State Baptist Convention.

This book is the outgrowth of my personal, Christian walk with God. It was deeply buried in my mind, experiences, feelings, and desire to spread the Gospel of Jesus Christ. I thank Dr. DaNita Weddle for providing the initial feedback, editing, and suggesting ideas for expanding the details of my journey.

I thank Mrs. Margo DeRamus for diligently teaching the Word of God.

I thank my Pastor, Rev. Dr. Lee C. and Sister Kimberly Winfrey of Partakers Church Baptist for moving from Chicago, Illinois to Detroit, Michigan seeking to follow their mission to serve God.

Thank you for encouraging me to dream again by your teaching, preaching, prayers and praise of God; thank you for your leadership, example, strength, and dedication to the people of God.

Finally, by the Grace of God and His infinite power, I thank the dynamic publishing team of Elizabeth Ann Atkins and her sister, Catherine M. Greenspan, of Two Sisters Writing and Publishing for taking on this project and creating the magical space to fulfill my dream. Your approach to coaching, leadership, publishing, and fostering great authors is impeccable. Thank you for the consultation, supervision, and explanation for everything throughout the process. I am grateful for your knowledge, enthusiasm, standards of excellence, and professional expertise.

Thank You So Much,
Regina Alexis DuBose

Bibliography

THE FOLLOWING SOURCES WERE used for my personal notes, quotations, and reference material in this literary work, and encouraged my spiritual growth. They are highly recommended to believers for continued maturity.

C. I. Scofield, D.D, *The New Scofield Study Bible, Holy Bible*, Authorized King James Version, (New York, Oxford University Press, 1967).

Bill Bright, *The Four Spiritual Laws,* (San Bernardino, CA: Campus Crusade for Christ; now Cru, 1965).

Dawson Trotman, *Lessons on Assurance*, (Colorado Springs, CO: The Navigators, NavPress 1975).

Bill Bright, *Ten Basic Steps Toward Christian Maturity,* (San Bernardino, CA: NewLife Pub., 1994).

Kenneth George Smith, Floy M. Smith, *Learning to Be a Woman,* (Westmont, IL: InterVarsity Press, 1970).

David Wilkerson, *The Cross and the Switchblade*, (New York, NY: Penguin Random House, LLC, 1962).

Bill Gothard Seminars, *Institute in Basic Youth Conflicts*, (Oak Brook, IL: 1974).

HARAMBEE, Sponsored by Cru (Campus Crusade for Christ), Various locations: 1976-1977.

Tim LaHaye, (*The Spirit Controlled Temperament,* (La Mesa, CA: Tyndale House Publishers, Inc., 1966).

Corrie ten Boom with John and Elizabeth Sherrill, *The Hiding Place,* (Grand Rapids, MI: Chosen Books, 1971).

Hannah Hurnard, *Hinds' Feet On High Places,* (United Kingdom: Bantam Books, 1973 Edition; Original: Christian Literature Crusade, 1955).

C. S. Lewis, *The Screwtape Letters*, (United Kingdom: Geoffrey Bles 1942).

Leslie B. Flynn, *19 Gifts of the Spirit*, (Colorado Springs, CO: David C. Cook, 1974).

Michael Pink, *The Bible Incorporated,* (Cleveland:Ohio; New York City: World Publishing, 1988).

Patricia Beall Gruits, *Understanding God and His Covenants,* (Rochester Hills, MI: Peterpat Publishing, 1985).

Drs. Jerry & Carol Robeson, *Strongman's His Name...,* (Kensington, PA: Whitaker House, 2000)

Ellis Orozco, Alice Stegemann, Byron Stevenson, Dennis Wiles, *14 Habits of Highly Effective Disciples,* (Dallas, TX: BaptistWay Press, 2014).

J. E. O'Day, *Discovering Your Spiritual Gifts,* (Downers Grove, IL: InterVarsity Press, 1985), pp. 11-15.

Kevin W. Earley, *Every Member Ministry: Spiritual Gifts and God's Design for Service,* (Anderson, IN, Warner Press, 2016)

Endnotes

1   J. E. O'Day, *Discovering Your Spiritual Gifts,* (Downers Grove, IL: InterVarsity Press, 1985), pp. 11-15. https://www.amazon.com/ Discovering-Your-Spiritual-Gifts-Booklets/dp/0877840717. Last accessed 9-17-21.

2   Kevin W. Earley, *Every Member Ministry: Spiritual Gifts and God's Design for Service,* (Anderson, IN, Warner Press, 2016). https://www. warnerpress.org/9781593176440every-member-ministry.html. Last accessed 9-17-21.

3   Patricia Beall Gruits, *Understanding God and His Covenants,* (Rochester Hills, MI: Peterpat Publishing, 1985). https://www.amazon.com/ Understanding-God-Covenants-Patricia-Gruits/dp/0935945008. Last accessed 9-17-21.

4   [4] Leslie B. Flynn, *19 Gifts of the Spirit* by, (David C. Cook, 1994). https:// www.amazon.com/19-Gifts-Spirit-Leslie-Flynn/dp/1564763374/ref= sr_1_1?dchild=1&keywords=Leslie+B.+Flynn%2C+19+Gifts+of+the +Spirit&qid=1631926250&s=books&sr=1-1. Last accessed 9-17-21.

CPSIA information can be obtained
at www.ICGtesting.com
Printed in the USA
BVHW021456041021
618103BV00002B/3